# DEFINITELY
# HISPANIC

# DEFINITELY HISPANIC

Growing Up Latino
and Celebrating What Unites Us

## LeJuan James

WITH CECILIA MOLINARI

**ATRIA** BOOKS
New York   London   Toronto   Sydney   New Delhi

**ATRIA**
BOOKS

An Imprint of Simon & Schuster, Inc.
1230 Avenue of the Americas
New York, NY 10020

First Atria Books hardcover edition June 2019

**ATRIA** B O O K S and colophon are trademarks of Simon & Schuster, Inc.

For information about special discounts for bulk purchases,
please contact Simon & Schuster Special Sales at
1-866-506-1949 or business@simonandschuster.com.

The Simon & Schuster Speakers Bureau can bring authors to
your live event. For more information or to book an event, contact
the Simon & Schuster Speakers Bureau at 1-866-248-3049
or visit our website at www.simonspeakers.com.

Interior design by Kyoko Watanabe

Manufactured in the United States of America

10 9 8 7 6 5 4 3 2 1

Library of Congress Cataloging-in-Publication Data

Names: James, LeJuan, author. | Molinari, Cecilia, author.
Title: Definitely Hispanic : essays on growing up Latino and celebrating what
   unites us / LeJuan James ; with Cecilia Molinari.
Description: First Atria Books hardcover edition. | New York, NY : Atria
   Books, an imprint of Simon & Schuster, Inc., 2019.
Identifiers: LCCN 2018042506 (print) | LCCN 2018055285 (ebook)
Subjects: LCSH: James, LeJuan—Childhood and youth. | Hispanic American
   youth—Social conditions.
Classification: LCC E184.S75 (ebook) | LCC E184.S75 J36 2019 (print) |
   DDC 305.235089/968073—dc23

ISBN 978-1-5011-9420-7
ISBN 978-1-5011-9421-4 (ebook)

*To my family and supporters.*
*I couldn't have done any of this without you.*

# CONTENTS

*Introduction* ▪ ix

1. #Home ▪ 1

2. #HispanicParenting101 ▪ 19

3. #LaPela ▪ 37

4. #CuandoYoMeMuera ▪ 53

5. #Education ▪ 57

6. #LifeLessonsAreEverywhere ▪ 67

7. #ReduceReuseRecycle ▪ 75

8. #SuperstitionsPremonitionsandHomeRemedies ▪ 85

9. #MusicIsInOurDNA ▪ 95

10. #FoodIsLove ▪ 103

11. #ElBochinche ▪ 109

# Contents

12. #HispanicFamilyGatherings ▪ 117

13. #MamáHayUnaSola ▪ 133

14. #DatingHispanicWomen ▪ 143

15. #RelationshipGoals ▪ 153

16. #Abuela ▪ 169

17. #TheHouse ▪ 181

18. #BecomingLeJuanJames ▪ 189

*Acknowledgments* ▪ 205

# INTRODUCTION

I've always loved making people laugh. And five years ago, I was blessed to discover that I could actually make people laugh and create a positive impact on their lives for a living by re-creating scenes based on my experiences growing up Hispanic in the United States. Everything from my childhood is so vivid—I can feel it, touch it, smell it. I close my eyes and can transport myself to when I was a kid following (or breaking) our strict house rules; dancing and arguing with my loving, fierce, and selfless mom; listening attentively to my kindhearted, tenacious, and caring dad; looking up to, admiring, and competing with my smart and passionate big sister; playing and becoming best friends with my beloved little brother; and hanging out with my dear, wise, and compassionate abuela. Those joyous, colorful, and sometimes dramatic memories are so strong and present in my mind that bringing them to life in my videos is only natural to me.

I am incredibly proud of being Hispanic. Everything that we represent as a community and as a people is rooted in our love for life, our respect for others, and our compassion and empathy.

Our households are much sterner than those of other cultures surrounding us, and although I suffered through it as a kid, I now understand that it is because our parents are looking out for us, teaching us important life lessons on a day-to-day basis because they simply want the best for us. From the outside, our homes may look like small dictatorships, but to us it's normal, it's our way of life. Some people may not get it, but every act of discipline, every rule, every lesson, every hug, every laugh molds us into better human beings, arming us with the tools we need to succeed in every chapter of our lives.

When I was living in my first apartment in a dodgy part of town, I never imagined that the short-form videos I was creating for fun would go viral and open this new and unexpected door in my journey. To be able to share my Hispanic heritage and each of these stages of my life with my viewers through these videos on different platforms and to make an impact on their lives is absolutely amazing. I get to showcase our culture and explore snippets of our reality not only to make you laugh and reminisce but also to keep our culture and traditions alive for future generations. And now I've been blessed with the opportunity to dive deeper into this exploration with this book.

I never really sat down to talk about and analyze our way of life at such a profound level before, but by doing so I have come to realize that I am not only proud but honored to be Hispanic. We see and experience life from our own unique perspective. Our tangible excitement and celebratory impulses when something goes well in our lives; our hotheaded and passionate reactions when facing roadblocks; our deep love and respect for the elders in our families and communities; the way we always look out for each other and extend a helping hand or a plate of food to anyone in need—each and every piece of the puzzle that makes us Hispanics, Latinos, Latinas, Latinx (or whatever label you prefer to use) is absolute and pure magic.

That's also why people from different Latin American countries can watch my videos and laugh wholeheartedly, because we've all been there. Those skits reflect our childhoods, and I hope that these pages will reflect our loud, expressive, and affectionate hearts. This book isn't about my videos, although you will be able to clearly see where some of the inspiration for them came from. This is a reflection on what makes us tick, and it is also me opening up to you—sharing my story, my thoughts, my perspective—so that we can go beyond my skits and travel down memory lane together, and through all the ups and downs and laugh-out-loud moments that come with being Hispanic in the United States.

I hope that no matter how old or young you may be, you too will be able to relate to the range of emotions in these pages and at long last understand that at some point in our growing up, we all thought our parents were nuts. We are all puzzled by some of our customs, rules, and disciplinary actions. And regardless of what Latin American country we may come from, we all share a common upbringing. Yes, we each have our own slang, specific traditions, and nuances, but we were raised on the same basic set of principles, an underlying and unifying thread sewn throughout our lands that bands us together.

So when you're getting yelled at as a kid, when you're getting a *chancla* thrown over your head, when you're doing chores on the weekend when you'd rather be playing videogames, when you suffer a *pela* for not following the rules, when you wish you were old enough to leave home, remember this: it all comes from pure, unconditional, and almighty love. Your parents love you, have faith in you, and want the best for you. We are a united front. Each Latin American country beyond our own is part of our extended family, sharing similar struggles and celebrations, and an unbreakable bond. We're loud and we're going to embarrass you. We may seem like we care too much, but it's never enough, because we love hard, we take pride in our families, and we will do everything in our power to make sure everyone in our circle is looked after. We aren't crazy, we're just Hispanic! Read on, enjoy, and use the hashtag titles to share some of your own personal stories and anecdotes on social media about these topics that are such key parts of the fabric of our glorious community.

# DEFINITELY
# HISPANIC

# #Home

I HAVE A PROFOUND love for Central Florida. Every time I fly back into Orlando I tell my fiancée, Camila, how happy I am to call this my home. The connection runs deep and has a stronger hold on me than I ever thought possible, especially since this wasn't my first home. I think that's what gives it an extra-special place in my heart. Had it not been for all the moving around, I may have not been able to appreciate this home as much as I do now. And I likely wouldn't be doing what I'm doing now on social media. The more years go by, the more I realize that everything happens for a reason; it's all part of God's plan.

My parents welcomed me into this world on February 19, 1990, in Providence, Rhode Island. Yes, you read right. I wasn't born in Puerto Rico or the Dominican Republic, and I wasn't born in Orlando. By a curious twist of fate, I was born in Providence, Rhode Island. Mami and Papi had moved there a year earlier from Puerto Rico searching for job opportunities and a better life for them and my sister, Nahil, who was born in 1988. As was quickly becoming characteristic in my family, they took a leap of faith and readily hopped on that plane toward an unforeseen future filled with hope. It didn't hurt that they had family members there too, who encouraged them to give Rhode Island a shot.

They settled in quickly, renting their own apartment and landing jobs at nearby factories. Mami was so excited about her first day on the job and was so eager to make a good first impression that she dressed to the nines in full business attire and strutted onto the premises ready to show them what she had to offer, only to realize that this was far from the appropriate outfit for such a hands-on position. Taken aback for a split second, she gathered herself, rolled up her sleeves, and got to work, ready and unafraid to get her hands dirty and do whatever was necessary to survive. As she gained ground at the factory, she began to bring other friends and family into the fold—like many Hispanics, always willing to lend a helping hand to those in need. And with her broken Spanglish, high-flying hand gestures, vivacious expressions, and good disposition, she managed to thrive in this new environment.

While my mom found her groove in her new job, my dad started working at another factory, and soon after transferred to the same one as my mom. After a slight adjustment period, which all immigrants in a new country are all too familiar with, everything began to fall into place. My maternal grandparents

## Where There's a Will, There's a Way

It always amazes me to see how Hispanics have a knack for communicating in the United States regardless of how much English they know. Where there's a will, there's definitely a way for us. It's a survival instinct, but it's also part of who we are. Hispanics are usually a friendly bunch. We love chatting, and if we can't figure out how to say something ourselves, we will not shy away from dragging other people into our conversations to help get our point across. *"Oye, tú, ven acá, ayúdame con esta vainita* and help me tell this man what I need."* If all else fails, our version of Google Translate is our wildly expressive faces and hand gestures, along with slowly mouthed words in Spanish, which mean nothing to an English speaker—*¿Dóondeee estáaa el toooiiileeet?*—but we assume saying it in slow motion will help get through to them. Somehow, miraculously, we make it work.

had moved to Rhode Island with them to help out with my sister, allowing Mami and Papi to both hold full-time jobs and provide for the family. Then I came along.

Once I was born, my mom left the factory on maternity leave and relished the precious weeks she was able to stay at home with her newborn baby and little girl. However, when the time came to rejoin the workforce, instead of going back to the factory, she decided to give real estate a shot and hit it out of the park. She was doing so well that my dad decided to join her—

she was the face, he was the muscle, and together they made the perfect team.

Life was treating them well, but my dad was sorely missing his home and his people. Rhode Island had been good to us; however, the culture shock was deep, and those ice-cold winters were no laughing matter. He had endured it all as best he could, trying to adapt to uncharted waters, but the warmth of his island was calling him back home.

My father is a gentle and kind man, with a great big heart and a quiet yet noble demeanor. He is a man of few words, but when he expresses himself, he does so clearly. And that's how the first of many moves in my life came to be. The pull to go back to his home was so strong that he finally buckled and told my mom it was time. She couldn't believe her ears. They'd worked so hard to build a life for themselves in Providence, even managing to reach financial stability while doing something they both enjoyed, but she also knew that her husband was unhappy, and that wasn't going to fly in the Atiles household. A happy home equals a happy family, so she said yes, and they packed up our belongings and called it a day, not knowing that they would be back in this town many years later under very different circumstances.

## Puerto Rico and Dominican Republic, Here We Come!

It was 1992, and we were back in Puerto Rico. Well, it was actually my first time living there, but at age two, for all I knew or remembered, I had never lived anywhere else. Camuy quickly became what I will always recall as my first home and my mecca for learning and assimilating my proud Puerto Rican heritage. This is where I ate my first cheese dogs, *empanadillas de pizza, pinchos, tripletas, mofongos,* and *quesitos.* It's also where I first bonded with my paternal grandfather. He was a commentator for minor league baseball, so he'd take me with him all over the island to the different games. I spent a lot of time with him and we became really close. In the process, I fell in love with baseball, a sport that still holds an important place in my heart.

Another thing that holds a special spot in my childhood memories from Puerto Rico is *limber,* a fruit juice frozen in a plastic cup that was like a little slice of heaven to my taste buds. Like at an American lemonade stand, *limber, pastelillos,* and other snacks were usually sold directly from people's houses. However, there were no permits, rules, or regulations, only housewives or elderly retired grandmothers running little side businesses from their home kitchens, with just a sign out on the front yard that said: LIMBER 50 CENTAVOS. Sometimes there weren't even signs; it was good old word of mouth. I loved *limber* so much, it became an obligatory after-school snack to refresh me from the Caribbean heat before I headed back home for the rest of the day.

When I wasn't with my grandfather or getting my *limber* fix, I was hanging out with my family. During the weekends, we'd either go to the beach or hop in the car with my parents and sister and drive two towns over to Plaza del Norte or Plaza

Atlántico. Those two malls were it. We'd go shopping, eat at the food court, go to the movies, and hang out at the local arcade. That was my spot. I have been a fan of videogames ever since those weekends spent playing at Time Out.

Then came the summers in the Dominican Republic. My maternal grandparents lived with us in Puerto Rico but went back often to their native Dominican Republic. Soon, my sister and I started joining them during our summer vacations. That's when I was truly exposed to the magic of that island and my Dominican heritage. It's also the place where I became a bit more street smart. Since my parents weren't with us, and my grandparents were more lenient, my summers in Santo Domingo exposed me to new experiences that turned into cherished lifelong memories.

My grandmother would cook up a storm—*mangú, sancocho, habichuelas con dulce*—and I'd spend most of my days with my cousins at the beach or baseball games, but mostly just hanging out on our block. That's where I learned how to play *vitilla*, which was similar to baseball but played with a stick for a bat and a bottle cap for a ball—my first lesson in how to be resourceful and make do with what you have. And that's where I also first tasted and became a fan of *chimis* (Dominican hamburgers), *yaniqueques* (a type of fried dough finger food), and *refresco rojo*, a.k.a. Country Club (a national fruit-flavored soft drink).

I was having the time of my life playing with my cousins and friends and discovering the joys of island life in both Puerto Rico and the Dominican Republic. Meanwhile, my dad landed a government job and my mom hit the ground running with a good position at an elementary school, which would later become the place where I would attend first and second grade. Even as a proud Dominican, my mom was quick to readapt to Puerto Rican life, but the emotional struggle was real. There was family drama left and right, yet she did her best to pay it no heed and keep her chin up, appreciating all the wonderful things God was giving us, especially the new addition to our family in 1996: my little brother, Bryan. His birth was the biggest blessing of my childhood. I was ecstatic to have a baby brother and couldn't stop imagining all the things we would do together once he was a little older, unaware that the scenes playing out in my mind would actually take place soon, but in a faraway land.

Five years passed, and after giving it a heartfelt try, Papi found himself disappointed and still searching for something that seemed emotionally unattainable on his old turf. So, one day, he turned to my mom and she knew it was time to pack up again and fly off to new horizons. These moves were not easy on her, but she was determined to make her husband and family happy, and if that meant crossing the sea and moving back to the United States, so help us God, that was what we would do.

## Next Stop: Orlando, Florida

The first move etched in my memory bank, the one I can recall to this day, is when we moved to Orlando, Florida, in 1997. I had been there once before, a year earlier, during a family vacation. Disney World is pure magic, and for me, as a six-year-old, it really was like being in the place where dreams do come true. So, when my parents told me we were moving there a year later, I couldn't believe my luck! *Oh my God, we're moving to Disney!* Of course, moving to Orlando didn't mean we would be living in Disney World, but a boy can dream.

The day of our arrival, when we drove down the streets of Orlando to our new home, I was even more amazed than I had been during our first visit, especially because I knew this time it was not a vacation, this was permanent; this was the place we would now be calling home. The memory is actually still so vivid and fresh in my mind that I can easily close my eyes and remember it as if it were yesterday. I stared out the window, absorbing my new surroundings, in awe of the spotless off-white sidewalks with Disney-perfect flower beds lining pristinely paved and smooth roads. Drivers respected the stop signs and traffic lights, and everything seemed organized and functioning like a well-oiled machine. When we reached our new house, carried our luggage inside, and settled into our rooms, I suddenly noticed I was no longer hot or sweaty. Back home in Puerto Rico, we had a small, rattling window AC, which we only turned on when the heat became unbearable, but in Orlando, the inside temperature was cool and comfortable, and as the hours ticked by, it never changed: the joy and wonder of central air-conditioning.

Living a hop and a skip away from Disney World, in a house where the AC was always on, walking down spotless streets, what more could a seven-year-old boy ask for? There was no real emotional toll accompanying this move for me—that would come later. This time around, it was like a big adventure in which I awaited every twist and turn with eager anticipation. And part of that adventure was my newfound relationship with my little brother. Despite the age difference, we quickly became inseparable. We shared the same room, hung out, and as soon as he was old enough, we started playing videogames and basketball, and he became my best friend.

Another part of that adventurous chapter in my life was facing a new school in a new language and making new friends. I had learned some basic English back in Puerto Rico, since it is a school requirement, but had never really practiced the language outside of the classroom. Fortunately, I wasn't alone. Our class was incredibly diverse—also a first in my life—with quite a few kids from different parts of the world, so many of us were in the same boat. I managed to get by with the essentials and picked up the rest of the language quickly—definitely quicker than my mom and dad.

As I adjusted to my American school and friends, my parents hit the pavement in search for jobs. They went straight to Disney's employment office and were handed applications to fill in by hand—which were all in English. Gotta love Hispanics! Unlike talking, which we will do with anyone and everyone, if we read something we don't quite understand, we'll be damned if we ask a stranger what it means. Call it pride or what you may, but we immediately assume that we can figure it out on our own—we got this—sometimes to our detriment. As my mom filled out her application—cruising through the basics like name, address, and so forth—she ticked off "Housekeeping" when she reached the list of possible jobs. Mami assumed it was some sort of homemakers' publication, like the magazine *Good Housekeeping*. My dad didn't fall far behind. While completing his application, he checked "dishwasher" as a possible position, assuming he would simply have to unload and reload a dishwasher and then press a button for it to do all the work. Boy, were they in for a surprise!

On her first day, much like her first day at the factory in Rhode Island, my mom walked into that Disney building wearing her favorite business suit and pumps, only to find out that *housekeeping* really meant cleaning the Disney resort hotel rooms, changing sheets, making beds, restocking the toiletries, and so much more. Clearly recognizing her mistake, instead of turning around and calling it quits or feeling that her well-educated self was better than this position, she faced the day head-on, much to her boss's surprise, and dove right in.

Mami took off her jacket, rolled up her button-down shirt's sleeves, and worked in lockstep with the woman assigned to train her. By the end of her shift, muscles she didn't even know existed were pounding with pain throughout her body. She was ready to drop from exhaustion, but she didn't give up. On the contrary, she got up every morning after that and faced each day determined to do her best for her family.

My dad's experience was no different. He arrived at work on his first day and was sent straight into the trenches to find stacks of dirty dishes and just a sink, a faucet, dish soap, and a

## Ride-or-Die

The term *ride-or-die* seems to literally define us as Hispanics. Our people cross deserts and roiling rivers, sail across the seas on makeshift rafts, and undergo endless life-threatening conditions, all for the mere possibility of providing their families with a better life. We are there for each other through thick and thin and are willing to make any sacrifice for the well-being of our loved ones. That is why we are also not above or below anything when it comes to work. A job is a job, and we are taught to fulfill our obligations in order to find success and provide for our family, no matter how hard the tasks at hand may be. Therefore, no job is too little or too big for us—and for those of us who didn't have to make such huge sacrifices, you better believe our parents and grandparents will remind us of this every single day. *"Tú no tienes idea lo que yo y tu mamá hemos hecho para que tú y tus hermanos puedan vivir como viven hoy."* Yeah, I've already heard the stories about the sacrifices my parents made for me to have the luxury of choosing what I want to do with my life. But that won't stop them from sharing those stories over and over again. There is no escaping this truth. It is so hardwired into our mind-set that it eventually becomes the driving force behind our work ethic. If you or your ancestors have sacrificed everything for the possibility of a better life, then you better believe that the job you are given is to be cherished and done to the absolute best of your ability. Nothing should or will stand in our way.

sponge to get the job done. Rather than cower away, he stepped up to the plate and put his hands to work without complaining. If that was what he had to do, then that was what he would do. After endless days and countless plates passing through his tired and dried-out hands, his quiet hard work paid off; he was promoted to managing the actual dishwashing machines, which also existed but had been a step above his pay grade.

That initial job was absolutely ruthless, but it gave my dad a new appreciation for anyone and everyone who has ever worked or continues to work in a kitchen. Those days are etched into his mind forever, and also became a handy resource he'd pull out to remind us kids how good we actually had it if he found us complaining about first-world problems.

Meanwhile, at school, I was being exposed to American culture for the first time. I quickly adapted to my environment, but it was also where I started realizing that we were different from the mainstream here. As a kid you don't fully realize there's anything other than the perspective you receive from your parents and grandparents about the world, until you travel or move to another country and see it for yourself.

The first time this realization hit me was the first time I had a playdate at a friend's house and was invited to stay for dinner. I was starving and ready for my usual feast of meat with rice and beans—you know, the usual spread at home. But man, was I in for a surprise! Before me stood a blob of bright orange-yellow creamy elbow pasta and a slice of yellowish bread that I had never seen before in my life. *This is all we're eating? There's no rice? No beans? Where's the rest of the food?* Mac and cheese and corn bread: a monochrome meal, a staple of the American diet, and an anomaly to my eyes. That was the first shocker. Then came others, like realizing that I would never be allowed to sleep over at my friend's house.

"But, Moooom, why can't I do it if all my classmates are doing it?" I'd protest.

*"Ajá, entonces, si todos se tiran por un puente, ¿tú también te vas a tirar?"* she'd say, annoyed at my oblivious complaining.

"No, Mami, I am not going to follow everyone off a bridge just because I want to go to a sleepover with my friends."

But what I said or thought didn't matter. It was against the rules and that was final. Rules. Yet another difference between Hispanics and the American culture I was trying to adopt. Our parents are so much stricter than the average American parent. We need to report ourselves constantly; we have chores to do and obligations to fulfill; and if they don't know where we are at all times of the day and we are not home by our curfew, we are in for the scolding of our lives, a.k.a. *la pela.* I'll get into Hispanic parenting later, but suffice to say, that first stint in Florida really opened my eyes to a different world. It helped me appreciate what we had at home, while also showing me that there were other ways of living, which weren't necessarily wrong, simply unlike what I had been exposed to up until then. Little did I know every detail I was absorbing would later turn into the centerpiece of my career.

As the years flew by, I reached an age where I began to form my own opinions and started thinking for myself. They were incredibly formative years, ones that I cherish immensely to this day. I made friends, bonded with my little brother, found my groove at school, became fluent in English, and made Florida my home. That's why, when my parents told us one night over dinner that we were moving back to Puerto Rico, I saw my perfectly happy life crumble before my eyes, and I exploded in a hissy fit of enormous proportions. *How could they do this to me?* Obviously, when you are twelve, everything that happens feels like it is done to you and only you on purpose. I didn't get the reasoning behind the move, I just knew it would affect *my* life, and I wasn't having it. I cried tears of rebellious rage, I kicked and screamed, and refused to leave my friends behind. But clearly that wasn't my choice to make. We were moving, whether I liked it or not.

The reason behind what I thought was the most devastating moment of my twelve-year-old life was a job offer my mom had received at the school where she used to work before we moved to Florida. Her old boss needed her help, and she decided to take her up on the job opportunity. This time, it was my mom who drove our move, not my dad. But he readily agreed, likely hoping that maybe one more try in Puerto Rico would make everything fall into place for us to stay there permanently. So, much to my dismay, I had to buck up and deal with the heartbreak of leaving my friends behind. But my woes did not last long. I had a soft spot for Puerto Rico, I always will, and as soon as we settled in and I started school in Villa Serena, Arecibo, I was back to joking around and making friends, hanging out, playing sports, and eating all my favorite dishes. It was actually easier than I had expected to readapt to the island because Puerto Rico was already a big part of who I was.

Two years went by, and I was nearing that age when school and your friends become your entire life. We hung out every day, talked on the phone nonstop, played and watched games together; we had our set routines, and I was all-around happy once again. Until that dreaded afternoon when my parents interrupted a videogame session in my room to sit me down and talk. That's when they broke the news: "We're moving back to Orlando." *Again? Whyyy?* Our time in Puerto Rico had come to an end, and they knew there were better opportunities for us in Florida; it was something to be done for the good of the family, but all I could think was *Why do we have to keep moving? Why can't we just stay put in one place? Why do I have to leave my friends again?* I was up in arms, furious at them. I refused to be uprooted another time, but none of that mattered. The decision had already been made, and I had to figure out a way to deal with it. I snapped back at them and felt so incredibly devastated and misunderstood. *How could they do this to me again?* And right when I was about to start high school!

I think many of you who have had to move around as kids can relate. We just don't get it at that age. Adult issues are so foreign to us that we can't see how dislocating our lives would do our family any good. I was just so blinded by my anger, I couldn't process the fact that my parents were really doing what was best for all of us, making a move that would determine our fates and gift us with possibilities beyond our wildest dreams.

At the time, it felt like the end of the world as I knew it, but now I know what seemed like my ultimate nightmare becoming a reality was actually a total godsend. Had it not been for all that back-and-forth, the struggles, the different schools, the new friends, the shifting languages, I wouldn't be who I am today. And without those experiences, without those decisions, without my family, I wouldn't be where I am today. Florida allowed me to understand American culture and assimilate certain aspects of it into my daily life. However, my Puerto Rican and Dominican roots run deep. This identity will never be lost to me. No matter where we were, my mom and dad always made it a priority to embed in us the traditions and cultures of these two amazing islands that make up my genetic pool. And it worked. Puerto Rico and the Dominican Republic are part of my heritage and a key part of the fabric of my life. I am blessed to feel very much Puerto Rican and Dominican, and I am also blessed to live in a country that allows me to be me and flourish in my own reality as a Hispanic growing up in the United States.

I get it. I get the culture shock we suffer when we first move here. I also get the plight of the first-generation kid who thinks his or her Hispanic parents are crazy and don't understand why they act the way they do. I get feeling misunderstood, and I also get feeling like an outsider. And that's exactly what has allowed me to do what I do on social media today. Had it not been for each one of these moves and experiences, and my colorful and beloved family, I would not have the wealth of content to share with my audience—content that celebrates every detail and nuance that makes us who we are as a Hispanic community, that hits home for many people because, in some way or other, we have all been there. What more could I ask for? Thank you, Mami and Papi. I wouldn't have it any other way.

# #HispanicParenting101

HISPANIC PARENTS RUN a really tight ship at home. Our upbringing is layered with tough love, support, and major crackdowns when we misbehave. It is an intricate, strict, rule-bound operation that aims to teach us discipline, respect, love, and compassion. But as kids, sometimes we feel our parents' methods are way too over-the-top, rigid, and ironfisted. Rules are meant to be broken, right? Not in our house! That saying couldn't be farther from our truth. We must abide at all times by this list of unspoken rules or face dire consequences. Some of the rules make sense to us as kids, and some seem completely bananas, but we dare not question them. Because although our parents will hear us out, in the end, they reign supreme. Whatever they say is the law of the land. There's really no way around this, so I'm here to help. In addition to the Ten Commandments, which serve as our moral compass, here are the top five rules Hispanic parents expect their children to obey at all times.

## Rule 1: Respect

Above all and no matter what, the number one rule that is embedded in our souls from the moment we are born is respect. We must respect our parents, our elders, our siblings, our neighbors, teachers, classmates, community, and we must respect the rules. Respect is so entrenched in our nature that one of our more common running phrases is *"¡Qué falta de respeto!"* which literally means "What a lack of respect!" It doesn't have as powerful a ring to it in English, but when we hear our parents utter these words, we know that we have crossed the point of no return and have to run to escape what will inevitably follow, the one moment we dread more than any other: *la pela* (which is too important to gloss over; so much so that you can read more about this deep-seated phenomenon in the next essay).

Our parents' obsession with respect is hard to swallow when we're kids and even more so when we're rebellious teens. Whatever we do feels like it's wrong and we just don't understand what they want or why they do what they do. If we get home late, we are disrespecting their preestablished curfew. If we don't do well enough at school, we are disrespecting their hard work to provide us with a solid education. If we get a tattoo, we are disrespecting our bodies. Every one of our actions could be interpreted as a form of disrespect. It can be stifling and frustrating, and has driven most of us to think at some point, *Oh my God, you are so annoying! ¡Déjame quieto!* However, as the years go by and we get a little older, their intentions become clearer. They are molding us into respectful, hardworking, and disciplined human beings. They are giving us all the tools we need to survive in the real world once we fly the nest. All they really want is for us to be happy and successful. How can we show our parents the respect they deserve?

1. Abide by their rules as kids and teens; they exist for a reason, even if you can't quite understand that yet.
2. Listen respectfully to their advice throughout your entire life (no one knows you better than your parents).
3. Give them a hand when you see them struggling, even when you're annoyed that they still don't know how to work their old smartphones.
4. Show them your gratitude; thank them for all the sacrifices they have made to give you a better life.
5. Love them with all you've got, because even though you roll your eyes when they pull the infamous *"Cuando yo me muera . . ."* one day they really won't be around anymore and you will miss them more than you can imagine.


## Rule 2: Laziness Is Unacceptable

*Laziness.* I don't think that word is even part of our vocabulary. And if it is, our parents will smack it right out of our minds, because if you have hardworking parents who have sacrificed everything to give you a better life, the last thing they will tolerate is your laziness. What does this mean exactly? Chores fill our every waking hour—there is always something that needs to get done ASAP. And if we don't hop to it, our parents will unravel into a frenzy of anxiety and a monologue chronicling how, without their backbreaking, lazy-free existences, we would not be where we are today. So come the weekend, sleeping in is out of the question. There is too much to do!

If I happened to make this mistake on a Saturday or Sunday, my bedroom door would fly open with a *"¡Qué buena vida la tuya, ah! Nosotros aquí limpiando y tú ahí. ¡Te me paras de la cama y te me pones a trabajar porque en esta casa hay que ser productivo!"* No, I wasn't sleeping in till noon. It was only nine in the morning, just a couple of hours later than usual, but if I didn't jump out of bed immediately, the monologue would've gone on for another half hour, listing the long hours my parents worked to pay the bills and put food on the table while all I did was go to school. "What are you tired from?" Best not to answer that question. If they don't sleep in, neither should we.

In Hispanic households, weekends are not meant for resting. They're meant for cleaning and going to church. My list of duties included raking the patio, tidying up my room, washing the car, and if I'd done all of the above, something else would be added to my chores, like moving furniture around. I would walk into a room and immediately see a vision flash before my mom's eyes, which was followed with something like "I want to move the bed." If it wasn't the bed, it was the couch. She was always searching for the perfect place for each piece of furniture, and it usually took a few tries before she felt she'd nailed it, but she couldn't do it alone. I hated the labor involved in all of this, but saying no was not an option.

I honestly didn't get why we had to devote every weekend to cleaning and chores. It made no sense to me, but there was no questioning this anti-laziness rule. Eventually, I devised a plan to sneak in a little videogame time for myself without getting reprimanded. The key: going out of my way to not run into my parents for as long as humanly possible without raising suspicions. Out of sight, out of mind was my go-to tactic. If they didn't see me, they wouldn't ask me to do any extra chores. Most of the time, I was successful, but not for long. Our parents are always up in our business, keeping an eye on what we're doing even when we think they're not, which leads us to the next rule.

## Rule 3: Privacy = Wishful Thinking

Closed doors? Not in our house. Personal unopened mail? Never. Unidentified phone calls? Impossible. "I have a right to my privacy," you say? Keep dreaming! There is no privacy in a Hispanic household when you're a kid or a teen. Privacy under our parents' roof is called wishful thinking. In my house, the doors were always open. If I happened to go to my room and quietly close my door, one of my parents would eventually come barging in, no knocking of course, to see what I was up to. Because, as we are taught from a young age, they have a right to enter our rooms whenever they feel like it, with no respectful tapping on the door or "Can I come in?" And forget about locking the door behind you—that was absolutely unacceptable, would be incredibly suspect, and could cause all sorts of commotion.

There were times when my parents even conducted random searches in my room, checking my drawers and closets for evidence of any suspicious items, like drugs. And they were not subtle about it. I think American parents may do these types of searches too, but they make sure to go unnoticed so as not to rile up their kids about breaching their privacy. There was none of that with me. I would walk into my room after school and know when my parents had been rummaging around because my things were blatantly out of place, and if I complained in any way about them invading my privacy, I'd get an *"Esta es mi casa, nene, y yo puedo hacer lo que me da la gana. Si no te gustan mis reglas, múdate,"* which basically boiled down to: their house, their rules. And if I couldn't deal with it, I should move out.

Phone calls also fell into the "they have the right to know" category. So if I happened to call a girl I liked and retreated to my room to talk to her in private, it was like my parents could smell it in the air. Five minutes into the conversation, I would hear my mom say, *"¿Con quién tú hablas?"* to which I'd reply, "Mami, I'm talking to a friend," hoping to get her off my back. *"¿Quién es tu amigo? ¿Yo lo conozco?"* she'd press on, which was my cue to whisper into my phone, "Look, I have to go, my mom is here," and then hang up. Then the grilling would begin. I think it was even worse for my sister because all eyes are on the girls in the family, making sure they are acting like respectable *señoritas,* especially when they reach dating age.

Even if we tried to keep something from our parents, or have a private conversation in another room, they would find out. I am convinced they have superpowers, including supersonic hearing. Or are you going to tell me you've never been in a situation where you talked back to your parents under your breath only to be whiplashed by their glaring eyes and a sharply and slowly pronounced, "What did you just say?" How do they do that? I attribute it to their sixth sense, that sweeping power with which they govern our lives and keep us on the right track.

---

### No English, *me haces el favor*

This is not a steadfast rule in every household, but it is common enough to deserve an honorable mention. Our parents have nothing against us learning English. On the contrary, they want us to excel at it because they know doing so will open many more doors in our future. But English at home is another story. If they come at you with something big or small, a personal issue, an unfinished chore, a crisis, and you start off your response in English, they will cut you off like a bad habit and go in on you: *"Espérate, espérate, ¿por qué tú me estás hablando en inglés? En esta casa se habla es-pa-ñol, mi amor. Espanish only."* And that is final. It really all comes down to them fearing that we will forget our native tongue—it may be annoying when you are a kid, but their intentions are solid, and you will thank them later, believe me.

---

## Rule 4: Obsessive-Compulsive Behaviors Are the Norm

Hispanic parents may not officially have obsessive-compulsive disorder, but sometimes it feels like they're only a few ticks away from a formal diagnosis. Think about it: Obsessive about dirt and contamination? Check! Obsessive need for order? Check! Obsessive about hoarding or saving? Check! Repetitive rituals? Check! Superstitious fears? Check!

Attention to detail and cleanliness is absolutely essential in our homes—it's practically in our DNA. I don't think you will ever walk into a Hispanic house and find it *patas arriba,* in disarray. It just won't happen. We take pride in our immaculate homes, no matter how much or how little money we may have. What does this mean for us as kids? A hounding like no other to keep our rooms tidy and leave no mess behind. When you wake up, you make your bed before going to school, and when you go to sleep, you put away your clothes or shoes before crawling into bed. No sock should be left on the floor, no toy out of its designated container. Any type of a mess is unacceptable and grounds for an argument. When I hung out with my American friends and saw the state of upheaval in their rooms, I couldn't help but think, *My mom would kill me!* If my mom walked into my room and noticed a T-shirt on the floor, the world would come to a stop until I picked it up and put it away.

One of the reasons behind this obsession could be the fact that our doors are always open for visitors. People are comfortable dropping by our homes, so we feel the need to be prepared for these unexpected guests at all times. The rule of thumb is: The house must be clean and some sort of snack must be at the ready. And this brings us to their next obsession: the decorative pieces that are absolutely off-limits for those of us actually living there. Do not, under any circumstances, casually stroll in and sit on the decorative couches or use the good dining room table. You should know better. Those pieces of furniture are for special occasions only. And don't get me started on those decorative hand towels in the bathroom! *"Estas toallas son de decoración para cuando vienen las visitas. Son lindas, son suaves y no están hechas para que tú me las maltrates con tus manos sucias."* That really drove me nuts. Why have towels hanging in the bathroom that are for decoration and guests only? Whyyy? It makes no sense to me. My quiet rebellion against these pesky little towels would drive me to, dare I confess, dry my hands with them, but then guiltily align them so that no one could tell the difference—no need to add more fuel to the fire.

Our parents' OCD inclinations sometimes go beyond the house and into unexpected territories, like water. I'm talking big bodies of water, like a pool, a lake, a river, or an ocean. When water is involved, our parents go berserk. "Stay close to the ledge, *¡que te vas a ahogar!"* "Don't swim too far out *¡que te van a comer los tiburones!"* *"¡Hazme el favor y quédate donde te pueda ver, niño!"* They need to have eyes on us at all times when we are in the water because their biggest fear under those circumstances is our imminent death by drowning. The fear of losing their kids to the water is so real and deep that if you don't heed your parents' warning, they will stand up, march right over to the water, waddle in, and pull you out by the arm or ear or whatever they can grab while aggressively muttering, *"¿Qué te dije? ¡Que te quedaras donde te puedo ver! ¿Qué es lo que tú quieres? ¿Ahogarte?"* wondering if your plan all along was to drown and die. As irrational as it may sound, it is all linked to their strong love for their children and their knowledge that their super parent powers can only do so much to keep you safe, so don't you dare go swimming beyond their line of sight or you can kiss that day in the pool goodbye.

## Rule 5: Hispanic Parents Are *Not* Our Best Friends

Hispanic parents are here to educate us and raise us into decent, respectful, hardworking people. They will be there for us through thick and thin, ready to lend a helping hand and share their advice and wisdom. But one thing is as crystal clear as the beautiful seawater surrounding my islands: our parents are not and will never be our best friends. Get that notion out of your head right now. As much as they suffer when they have to reprimand us, as hurt as they may feel when in our teens we turn around and tell them we "hate" them, they will push through for our well-being and do whatever it takes to raise us right, and that does not include becoming best friends.

For Americans, the border between being their kids' parents and being their best friends is oftentimes blurry. That is not the case in our homes. Listen, this doesn't mean that we aren't close with our parents, that we don't share our feelings and confide in them. I talk or text with my parents on a daily basis. I seek them out for advice more than I do my own friends because I know they honestly have my best interest at heart. I also know that they will be straightforward with me and tell me the truth, even if it's not what I want to hear. However, there is a pronounced line drawn in my mind that I know should never be crossed. After all, at the end of the day, our parents are the ones who lay down the law in our land, and there is a certain amount of intimidation and straight-up fear that they instill in us as kids that lives on until the day we die.

It circles back to our first rule: respect. Our parents are not fazed by the fact that we may not like them sometimes, so long as we respect and love them. No matter how close we may be with our parents, we never lose that level of respect for them. Because our parents are not our equals. They are the people who will teach us our most valuable lifelong lessons; they are the ones we look up to; they are our leaders in this threatening and crazy world. Now that I am older, I understand this position and realize this is how I will likely be one day with my own children, because it works. I'm cool with my parents. In many areas, as we all grow older together, they are like friends; but unlike my friends, they are always going to call me out on stuff they think is wrong and put me in my place when I've lost my way. Our roles are so deeply rooted that the minute I spend time at home with my parents, they start acting like I am still living under their roof, criticizing and ordering me around, and I just have to grin and bear it because they are and forever will be my mom and dad first.

Just as our parents are not our friends, they sure have opinions about who we choose to hang out with! *"Dime con quién andas y te diré quién eres"* is their motto when it comes to friendships; you will be judged by the company you keep. And they take the *"dime con quién andas"* very seriously. When we bring a new friend over or simply mention a new name, our parents mutate into private detectives and immediately pounce on us with a series of questions that we must be prepared to answer:

1. Who are their parents?
2. What are their full names?
3. Where do they live?
4. How are they doing in school?
5. What kind of crowd do they hang out with?

If they could find out blood type, medical history, and criminal record without looking like they have lost their minds, they would. It is vital for our parents to gather as much information as possible about each one of our friends so as to know who we are surrounding ourselves with at all times. And this is just stage one in their investigation. Stage two is pure instinct. After meeting a new friend, my mom has an immediate hunch, based on a vibe or an energy—she just knows if that person will be good company for me or not. Call it intuition, her sixth sense, or what you may, it is off the charts, and she isn't afraid to be outspoken about it. *"Hmmm, a mí no me gusta ese muchachito..."* To which I usually replied, "Mami, stop being so dramatic." I was generally good at picking my friends, but I did have certain buddies who I thought were cool but were not liked by my parents. And without their approval, those friendships were sooner or later doomed because I wouldn't hear the end of it.

"I don't like him. *No me gusta para nada.* I don't want you hanging out with him anymore," my mom would say over and over again.

"Well, I don't care, he's my buddy. My friends are my life," I'd reply, a teenage knee-jerk reaction to her unshakable determination.

*"Los amigos son un peso en el bolsillo,"* my dad would chime in, calmly repeating his favorite catchphrase so as to drive the point home that friends are here one day and gone the next. I listened, but my teenage self didn't quite grasp this concept. I honestly thought my friends would be part of my life forever and that my parents just didn't understand. But he'd continue, as if reading my mind, "Don't think they are your life, because they can turn on you or leave when you least expect it."

It really is the last thing we want to hear as kids about our best friends, because we see them as our chosen family, the people who will have our backs through thick and thin. As teenagers we lean on our best friends, we depend on them, we want to talk and be with them 24-7 because we identify with them. And that is exactly why our parents grow so concerned and become so involved in the group of people we choose to be around. The fact is, they are older and wiser and they know how gullible and easily swayed we can be during those formative years. One of their main worries is us succumbing to peer pressure, which is why they always interrupt any of our "but my friend is allowed to do this" complaints with the classic *"¿Si tu amigo se tira por un puente, tú también te vas a tirar?"* which only serves to exasperate our misunderstood teenage souls. But our parents are not moved by how annoyed we are, all they care about is making sure we're with the right group of people, safe, and away from all the drugs and violence in the world. Sometimes they're successful at keeping us from the bad seeds, sometimes they're not, but their intentions are always solid.

As I got older and grew apart from many of the people I'd thought were my best friends, I finally understood where my parents were coming from. And although I had once been just as irked as any other teenage boy by their disapproval, time usually proved their intuitions right. The few friends that my parents didn't like from the get-go actually ended up making wrong choices later in their lives and going down shady paths. *How did they know?* It remains an unsolved mystery, but one that I will no longer question.

Even if our parents have conducted a thorough investigation of our friends and have deemed them appropriate in our lives, even if they actually like them and their families, sleepovers remain adamantly forbidden. I found this out the hard way during my middle school years, when sleepovers were a big thing. *"¿Para qué tú quieres ir a dormir en casa ajena cuando aquí tienes tu cama?"* The answer was always no. In truth, my parents didn't have a problem with the actual sleepover, they just wanted to make sure they could keep an eye on me, so sometimes I'd get lucky and they'd counteroffer with *"Invítalos para acá."* If having my friends over was the only solution, I would take what I could get.

Getting permission to go out with friends was another big ordeal. One of my early videos depicts this. When friends ask me to go out with them, and I stop in my tracks and say, "No, I have to ask my mom."

"What do you mean, you have to ask your mom?"

"Yeah, I can't just go out. I have to ask for permission."

It's hard to explain, but the whole "Hey, Mom, I'm going out," and her replying calmly, "Okay, be back by nine!" does not fly in our households. I had to start hinting at the possibility of going out a week before the actual day arrived to let it sink in with my parents. Then I knew what would follow would be the twenty questions, including who, what, where, when, and how, which I would have to diligently and patiently answer if I even wanted to dream of getting an okay from them. At long last, when my parents actually gave me the go-ahead, it was always under their relentless conditions, like a strict curfew regardless of whether it gave me time to hang out with my friends after a movie. And I had to painstakingly abide by those conditions if I ever wanted to go out again. Meanwhile, not only did my sister have to go through this same process, but if there were boys involved or it was any kind of date, my parents would immediately add, "Take your brother with you." Mind you, I'm two years younger than my sister, but my parents felt at ease with my presence "chaperoning" these situations, hoping it would help prevent any misbehaving on my sister's part.

All of my parents' tactics actually felt normal while we were in Puerto Rico, because every other kid went through the same scenario, but when we moved to the United States, it was another story. I couldn't help but compare myself and my life to my American friends and their lives, and the differences were so enormous and widespread that sometimes it felt really isolating. That's one of the reasons I'm here, with my videos and this book, because I know how you feel and I want to let you know that you're not alone. It happened to me while I was growing up in Orlando, and I didn't even have social media as an outlet or a source of information to accompany this awkward and misunderstood stage in my life. None of my friends had the same strict upbringing, so they couldn't relate or understand, which sometimes made me feel like an outsider. And I too often thought, *Yo, my parents are crazy. This is nuts. Why are they like this? Why can't they be like normal parents?*

The thing is, our parents are normal, just not normal by American standards. What we go through with our parents actually isn't weird at all; it is the norm in most of our Hispanic households. There's a method to their madness. That's why so many people can relate to my videos. I see your comments, those of you who feel relief when you realize you're not alone and your parents are just like mine, and those of you who reminisce about having experienced similar scenarios. And I just love it. Being able to provide this sense of community through my own memories and jokes is an absolute blessing.

What we all have to remember when our parents are going at us again and again and we feel they're pushing us over the edge is that there's a beauty to their actions that we will sooner or later come to appreciate. Why? Because as we grow and learn, we also realize that everything they do to us, all those rules they so adamantly enforce, is actually not *to* us but *for* us, and it stems from deep and unconditional love. And as we grow and learn, their words and advice take on new meaning and we start to take them into consideration, thinking: *Wait a minute. Are they right? Should I not do this?* There's an undeniable weight to their words, and their voices live on in our minds long after we've flown from the nest and started our adult lives. My mom will still, to this day, tell me when she doesn't approve of what I'm doing or saying or posting, and I honestly listen because my mom's and dad's opinions are key in my life as a grown man. Their approval has taken on a new and important meaning of providing guidance and respect.

Our parents are and forever will be deeply involved and invested in our lives. We are their most prized possessions, the light in their eyes. They know our interests, our moods, our passions, and I thank God and cherish every minute of my parents' existence, embracing them as much as I can and being there for them in their times of need as they get older. And you know why? Because they created this appreciation, respect, and love with their own love, discipline, and unconditional support. We are so lucky! I can't speak for other ethnicities and cultures, but the relationship between parents and their kids in the Hispanic community is truly an unbelievable, unique, beautiful, and unbreakable bond that should be cherished for the rest of our lives because, without them, we would not be who we are today.

# #LaPela

ALL RIGHT, WE'RE about to get down and dirty on a subject all too familiar and relatable to those of us who grew up or are growing up in Hispanic homes . . . the big, all-encompassing, and almighty *pela*. Let me break it down for those of you who've never had to endure a *pela* and have no clue what I'm talking about. The *pela* could be interpreted as the spanking's first cousin. They both serve the same purpose—to punish a child or teen for misbehaving, they both create the same sense of absolute apprehension and dismay, and they both sting. However, a spanking requires a parent to use his or her bare hand as the chosen disciplinary instrument while a *pela* involves a *correa* (belt) or a *chancla* (flip-flop, slipper, or slide). That's right, a *pela* has specific tools of the trade to help get the job done. Moms usually go for the *chancla* because it's more accessible to them, and dads tend to go for the *correa* for the same reason. Those are the two weapons of choice. Although sometimes parents are caught off guard and have to improvise and throw a spoon or hanger our way just to get the point across. Regardless of what tool they use, the minute we see a *chancla* or *correa* wielded, we know it is time to run for our lives.

Yet there seems to be a big misconception regarding *la pela*. Since we laugh and make fun of it openly, people tend to believe that we are getting *pelas* left and right for any old reason. But this is not the case. The truth is *la pela* is our parents' last resort, the one they turn to after exhausting all other options. Discipline and respect are the building blocks of our moms' and dads' parenting plan. There are strict rules to be followed and consequences to be met when we break these laws. From the moment we start crawling, one of the first words we register is *no*. Because our parents aren't about to let a baby, toddler, child, or teen do whatever he pleases under their roof. They are the leaders of the family pack, and they will make it known to any new family member from the very beginning. That *no* is what starts to draw the map of rules for us as kids. It shows us what we can and can't do. It sets boundaries that we learn to respect and follow. And it teaches us that when we disregard these rules and boundaries, we will get in trouble.

As kids, we learn through personal experience, so it is only natural for us to push these limits, cross a few of these boundaries, break some of the rules, and test our parents' patience, because by doing so we are figuring out the ropes of this so-called life we're discovering. We don't understand that we are never going to top our parents in an argument, because when we think we have them with our wit and reason, they will shut us down with an "I am your mother and there's nothing you can do about that." A response that can be infuriating, especially to preteens and adolescents, who think we know ev-ery-thing! So when we pull the wrong face at the wrong time, when we give attitude and talk back, when an argument gets heated, when we display any form of disrespect, when we cross that forbidden line, that's when *la pela* rears its ugly head. Yet before reaching this flash point, there are telltale signs, cues, and clear warnings offering escape routes and emergency exits from the one-way ticket to *pela* town.

## The Look

First up is the look: that one irrefutable and unique look that requires no words because we just know. It comes with a sudden yet minuscule silence in the room, a quick yet perceptible deep inhalation, and a glance in our direction that quietly yells, "Stop doing that right now . . . or else!" Sometimes it works, and we all go along our merry way, but other times we feel brave or are naïve enough to defy this first sign and continue doing whatever is getting under our parents' skin. That's when we get the second look, "You are crossing the line and you know it." We do know it by this point, but some irrational part of our brains urges us to keep going. Why? Because we are testing our boundaries and figuring out what we can get away with—not something we quite understand as kids, though. That's when the last of the three looks is launched in our direction, an expression that takes hold of a parent's entire face, the final brief and ominous glare that says, "You better start running." If I had a friend over, and I received this final unspoken reprimand, I would immediately turn to my buddy and say in a hushed voice, "Listen, you better go. I'm in trouble." He'd turn to me, puzzled, and reply, "What do you mean? How do you know?" to which I'd say, "I just know, you better leave now."

## The Voice

The vocal warning includes a slight shift in tone and volume mixed in with a few choice words. It is the child's responsibility to pick up on how irate the parent may be based on the combination of these three factors. It could just be a slight emphasis on a word that usually is used as a term of endearment, such as *"Mi ammmorrrr, ¿te puedes quedar quieto?"* Although it is formulated as a question with a *"mi amor"* thrown in there, the tone of voice is contained, the volume is low but poignant, the words are clearly pronounced and emphasized, and the question is actually intended as a statement: "You are embarrassing me in front of my new friends or the other customers in the store and need to behave and stay still *now.*"

Then come the outright blatant statements, with a slightly harsher tone and elevated volume, usually delivered in front of closer acquaintances or family: *"Te estoy diciendo que te quedes quieto, que te comportes . . ."* followed by *"¿Qué te pasa? ¿Tú no entiendes lo que te estoy tratando de decir?"* And when all else fails, the child gets the no-holds-barred warning sign of clear and present danger: *"¡Para de correr si no quieres un chancle-tazo!"* and the final nail in the coffin, one's full name: *"Juan Ricardo Atiles Tejeda."* By then, I would pretty much start writing my obituary because I knew all bets were off.

## The Countdown

Our parents are straight shooters. They will give us the looks, they will state their discontent with the utmost clarity, they will even give us first and second strikes, and sometimes, if they're in luck, we're receptive, and it works—even more so when we've already been through our share of *pelas*. But their methods do not include sitting us down and trying to reason with us by passively explaining why we should behave, because they know that we just won't get it. How do they know? Because they've been in our shoes when they were kids.

When a parent and a child do not see eye to eye, when the communication has surpassed all logic and reason, there's really no point in talking anymore. If you are disrespecting your elders, if you're talking back, if you're causing mayhem and not heeding all the cues, then there's no "Listen, Billy, we have to talk about what is going on here. I think that we can do better," because our parents know it will go in one ear and out the other. When things have escalated to this point, the truth is there are no words that will snap us out of our funk, our attitude, or our disobedience. We are so heated and blinded by our tantrums that we become our own undoing, and all our parents have in their bag of disciplinary tricks is one last fair warning: the countdown.

"I'm going to count to three," states your mom, plainly giving you one final signal urging you to turn around before plunging into the depths of *la pela*. "One!" she continues, loudly and firmly, while thinking, *I really hope I get through to this kid.* "Two!" she yells sternly, as you begin slowing down and realizing that it is now or never. You have one last chance to start behaving or you can continue to defy her authority until you reach the dreaded . . . "Three!" You are doomed. Now no amount of begging for forgiveness or praying for a miracle will get you out of the hole you just dug for yourself: You have officially entered *pela* territory. God have mercy on you.

## The Point of No Return

It's done. There is no turning back. You have pushed your luck and no number of apologies and pleading for clemency will remove you from *pela* territory. It is time to run for your dear life, take cover, and wait. Yes, wait. Because no hiding spot, no matter how ingenious, will deter this punishment. It is only a matter of time. And the more you challenge your parents, the worse it will become. I remember these cliffhanging moments like they were yesterday. My mom is fire and my dad ice. While she blew up, he remained calm, assessing the situation. They complemented each other well, so while my mom raged on, my dad would simply stand by, patiently waiting for his cue, and once he got the look from my mom, he would grab his belt, like a henchman about to carry out a sentence. I would sprint pointlessly and aimlessly around the house, bypassing dead ends while sidestepping, swerving, ducking, and dodging my dad's attempts to catch me with my matrix-like moves to no avail. My mom was never far behind, and many times she was the one at the helm of this disciplinary ship with her *chancla* looming above her head or a belt she'd expeditiously grabbed from the bedroom menacingly snapping between her hands.

*"¡Por favor, Mami, te juro que me voy a portar bien!"* I'd plead, promising to behave if she didn't hit me.

*"¡Es que yo soy la madre, y tú eres el hijo! ¿Cuántos años te va a costar entender eso? ¡Dime!"* she'd reply, letting me know that she was the mother and I was the child, and there was no turning back from what was to follow.

And that's when I felt the first snap on my leg. Shocked into submission, I'd cover my face and wait for the remaining whooping, because trying to grab the *correa* or *chancla* in that instance would only make matters worse. I know what you're thinking: *Oh, hell no, you should never grab the belt!* Even so, when I got a little older and had the audacity to defend myself, I would do that all the time, but no good ever came of it.

The fact of the matter is that, although this entire ordeal feels like the end of the world, it really only goes on for a minute tops, with two or three swipes of the *correa* or *chancla* to send a loud and clear "snap out of it" message, and then it's over. In truth, all you really feel on a physical level is a brief stinging sensation where you got hit. There are no lifelong scars or blood, just a bruised and battered ego and a sense of total defeat.

However, this didn't stop me from pulling out all the dramatic stops when *pela* time came a-knocking. When I was a kid in Puerto Rico and I saw my mom reach for the *chancla* or *correa*, I would beeline out the door and into the backyard screaming at the top of my lungs, *"¡Me van a maaataaar!* They're going to kill meeee!" Meanwhile, my mom would stand at the threshold, staring at her insane kid yelping and hollering, knowing full well that the neighbors were already aware of my dramatic antics to get out of a *pela*. Nowadays, my mom laughs when she tells this story—"Before we even laid one finger on you, you were already running around screaming bloody murder"—but she sure wasn't laughing back then.

Later, when I hit my early teens, my foolhardiness led me to say stuff like "This is cruelty. I'm gonna call the cops on you, the social service workers." As soon as those words exited my mouth, my parents would duck out of the room and reappear with the phone in their hands, wave it in front of my face, and say *"Llámalos.* Go ahead, call them, so they can take you to a foster home and you can see what's good." I was clearly bluffing in the hope that this threat would stop them, but they could see right through me and always replied with these smart comebacks that would silence me instantly and force me to think through the consequences of my empty threats. I hated these *pelas* like any other kid, but when it came down to it, I knew I lived in an all-around happy home and good environment and wasn't willing to give that up so easily.

And, come on, let's be honest, most of the time we knew that we were at fault from the start. Because the *chancla* didn't come flying into our faces out of nowhere and the *correa* wasn't whipped out for no reason. We'd usually pushed our luck and helped escalate an argument or situation to this boiling point, exhausting all our other options in the process. Hispanic parents don't want to resort to *la pela*, but when they feel cornered, that is all they have left in their disciplinary arsenal.

I should know. I went head to head with my mom for several years, mainly from when I turned eleven years old through my junior year in high school. That was the time span of our biggest disconnect, my so-called rebellious streak, even though it didn't involve misbehaving out on the streets, running with the wrong crowd, or flunking out of school. I would get in trouble for breaking a house rule, not listening when asked to do something, but above all for talking back to my mom. Although I was generally a good kid, I got into endless amounts of trouble with my mom because I could not hold my tongue. I know this may come as a surprise, because when you see us in our videos and the complete and unconditional love we have for each other, you'd never imagine we went through such a rough patch. But we did, and those years were tough for both of us.

To our detriment, I inherited my mom's fiery temper. So when we disagreed about something, our arguments went from tepid to scalding hot in the blink of an eye—like when I jumped in to defend my dad during an argument the two of them were having because I couldn't stand him remaining quiet and just taking it (little did I know that was his tactic to deal with her temper all along!). At that point, she'd forget what she was fighting about with my dad and turn her attention to me. It would start small, with a warning or reprimand, but her choice of words would set me off even more, prompting me to talk back, and in turn igniting her already steaming temper like a lighter in a parched forest.

Mami had met her match with me. My father has more passive inclinations; he is super low-key and opts to not engage when my mom gets mad. He's learned through their years together that it's best to let it go and talk about the issue at stake later, once my mom has calmed down. And she was used to this exchange, hence her surprise when her little boy stopped taking her outbursts standing down. When I found my voice in my early teens, Mami and I were suddenly in new and unfamiliar territory. I was adamant about expressing my two cents regardless of whether I was right or wrong, and this insubordination drove her bonkers and was immediately met with *la pela*.

*Why do they treat me this way? Why am I always getting in trouble?* I often wondered. Part of the problem was a lack of communication between my mom and me, or more likely the fact that we are so alike. I didn't think before I spoke and instead allowed my hotheadedness and rash responses to get the better of me. Meanwhile, my mom never stopped to think that I was really just like her. She didn't think about alternative ways to handle my rebellious streak because when she gets mad, she hunkers down, like a bulldog clamping down on its prey. There is no way to pry open that jaw once it's locked into place. When all is said and done, you can't put fire out with more fire. Something had to give, and the altercation was usually resolved with a *pela*.

Listen, it's not like our parents take pleasure in whooping us. Physical reprimand is not the first disciplinary step; it's their last resort, and it's an intricate part of our upbringing. That's why so many people react with laughter, recognition, and reminiscence when they see my videos on this topic. If you're Hispanic, the likelihood of your having gone through at least one of these scenarios is very high. You've been there. You know the drill. Running into your room, audaciously closing the door before they come at you, attempting to grab the belt before it hits you, knowing full well that all these responses will only aggravate the situation.

Is it fun? Hell no! Do we like it? Of course not! Does it serve a purpose? Yes. It's not like we're being beaten until they draw blood, though we may act like that in the heat of the moment. *La pela* is just a tool to jolt us into compliance and teach us right from wrong. In the end, our parents only want the best for us, and they know that this includes disciplining us when we don't know any better.

This is my truth, this is what happened to me. I'm fully aware that some people may see this differently or may have another experience, but it hasn't scarred me; I think it has actually worked to my benefit. My parents always made sure to talk to me once the pandemonium had died down, once my snappy attitude eased and I'd had enough time to process what had just happened. Disciplining their kids was not easy, they too felt bad, so they wanted to make sure it wasn't in vain. It was important for them to share the lesson behind the *pela* so as to prevent future altercations. As kids, we don't get it sometimes, and we hold a grudge, but those lessons are saved somewhere in our brains and prove to be useful when we least expect it.

I didn't like my heated arguments with my mom any more than she did, and once I realized that many of them stemmed from our similar personalities clashing, I decided to take a page from my dad's playbook and approach the situation from a new angle. If my mom couldn't stop our confrontations from escalating, then I would have to figure it out on my own. My first move was to attempt to take the high road, when the embers were burning between us, by biting my tongue, dousing my combustible temper, and controlling my own reactions. At first it was difficult, but as I practiced, it became easier, and our relationship reaped the benefits, though not without facing one last bump in the road.

I was twenty years old, attending community college, still living at home, and although our altercations had become fewer and farther between, that day Mami and I had another rattling blowup and it pushed me over my limit. On an impassioned impulse, while my parents were at work, I packed my belongings and, without giving it a second thought, moved out. I said nothing to my parents, I just grabbed my stuff and left the house. I'd never thought I would go through with it, that threat I dangled in front of my mom every time we fought when I was a teenager: "I can't wait till I'm eighteen so I can just move out already." In hindsight, I realize I didn't think it through, I let my emotions and hot-blooded temper get the best of me, and reality gave me one of the first *pelas* of my young adult life.

I stayed at a friend's house for a stretch, while I pinched

pennies and managed to save enough money to rent my own place. I struggled and felt somewhat lost at times, but I wasn't about to give up or go crawling back home. Eventually, my parents stepped in and helped me search for my first home away from home, forgiving me for such an abrupt exit in the process. The real adulthood I had unknowingly thrust myself into was a complete eye-opener. I suddenly understood just how hard life can be, how you have to make ends meet every month to pay the rent and the bills, how you get home from work tired and have to cook and clean up after yourself. It was the humbling experience the remains of my rebelliousness needed in order to at long last truly appreciate my parents and everything they had done for me. And that's when it hit me. I no longer felt the need to talk back and fight my mom; my stance with her softened and my understanding for my parents expanded. All those years I had felt my mom had been so hard on me growing up, but in that moment, I thought, *Oh, this is all worth it. I get it now.*

My dad used to always say, *"Hijo fuiste, padre serás,"* which was his way of telling me, "Look, you don't understand me right now, but when you have a kid of your own, you're going to get it." He was right, I didn't grasp the concept at the time. It took years until it finally clicked. Nobody tells us when we're kids that our parents come down hard on us in order to educate us and because they want the best for our lives. I personally didn't get it either until I was older and out of the house. I'm not a father yet, but I most definitely have a better understanding of what my dad meant with his saying. I know some of you may be reading this right now and not getting it either, but trust me, one day you will.

And guess what? I wouldn't change any of it because, together, we have grown. My mom's and dad's parenting skills have allowed me to become the man I am today. And each and every experience with them—the good, the bad, and the ugly—now serves as an inspiration for my comedy. It's a way of working through all our ups and downs and sharing them with the world to help you feel understood and comforted too.

In the end, the boundaries, the rules, the discipline, the *pelas,* and the post-*pela* speeches are all preparing us for the world outside the bubble that is our home. They're part of a bigger picture. The lesson instilled through our *pelas* is that our actions have consequences. Therefore, when faced with a shady situation or peer pressure as a vulnerable teen, knowing that a wrong decision might result in a *pela* will make us think twice before buckling. A common thought bubble that pops up in our minds is *I can't do that because I'm going to get in trouble,* which many times allows us to choose a healthier path for ourselves and our lives.

The seeds our parents are planting in our minds through their actions-have-consequences methods lead us to respect our elders, to abide by the rules, and to take responsibility for our actions. The world is not all sweet and dandy. There's also an ugliness that we will have to face the minute we step outside, and our parents' goal is for us to be as equipped and prepared as possible to survive that chaos. If you grow up in a bubble where you never fail, you are never reprimanded, and you never fall, you don't learn how to deal with these situations, and you don't learn one of the most vital lessons of them all: life in itself is full of *pelas*. If you're knocked down out in the real world, you have to get back up, dust yourself off, learn from your mistakes, and try again in order to eventually succeed.

# #CuandoYoMeMuera

I T'S A MOM THING, a dad thing, and even a grandparent thing. Every one of these members of your family will at some point resort to their own deaths to guilt-trip you into doing what they are pleading for you to do. Guilt trips are part of every Hispanic household. They are part of our religious culture. Guilt will drive you to confess and become a better person, but mixed up with the possible imminent death of a loved one, it's a game changer.

Hispanics are comfortable with death. Some of our countries choose to celebrate their dead loved ones, and we all talk about those who have passed and manage to keep them alive in our memories and our hearts through endless stories and anecdotes passed on from generation to generation. We are so comfortable with death that our parents will never shy away from using it to their advantage in hard-to-win arguments—and it works every time. If our moms or dads—especially our moms, though—feel that they have pulled out all the stops but are still failing to get through to us, they will unabashedly play the death card, and we are instant goners.

"*Cuando yo me muera* (when I die), you're going to wish you had kissed me and told me you loved me more often, but I won't be around anymore." How are you supposed to respond to that? There is really no way to come back from such a blow. What kind of rebuttal do you apply to death? It is the mother of all guilt trips. The last thing you want is to have your parents die or to even think about that possibility, especially when you're a kid. Nevertheless, that is an intricate part of my life. I can get hit with this phrase on any given day like a surprise attack. Even after I grew to identify this tactic, and rolled my eyes thinking, *Ugh, not this again,* I would do whatever was asked of me because it still pulled at my heart strings and made me feel bad. *What if she's right? What if she does die suddenly and I have to live with this guilt of not making her happy for the rest of my life?* Better to be safe than sorry is my philosophy in these circumstances.

Let me put this into perspective. Could you imagine watching an American sitcom and suddenly hearing the TV parents say to their children, "When I die, you're going to wish I was still around to take care of you, so you better finish your homework and be more respectful toward your father and me." That's right, follow the rules for no other reason than the fact that your parents are going to die. Sounds strange when you take it out of context, but for those of us in the Hispanic community, it's as common as rice and beans.

Usually when our parents threaten us with their peril, it's just to drive a point home. Most of the time it's about respect and lessons that they want to get through our hard young heads. Other times it's because they're feeling unappreciated. My mom would mainly use this phrase to scold me and make me feel guilty. She still pulls it out of her pocket every so often to get her way, and sometimes uses a variation: "I'm not getting any younger . . ." This one implies that she is hoping to have grandkids, ASAP. Talk about putting on the pressure!

For many years, I figured Mami simply didn't get how this phrase really affected us, and the intensity carried in those words. They're a constant reminder that she will not be around forever, *"Cuando yo me muera, te voy a hacer mucha falta, y ahí te vas a arrepentir."* This statement plays not only on our guilt but on the regret we will feel if our parents do happen to die before we comply with their request. It creates a sense of urgency, a need to get whatever they're asking for done as soon as possible. I've heard this so many times from my mom that one day I finally decided to ask her about it during a TV interview posted online. I imitated her *"Cuando yo me muera"* phrase and told her that it always made me feel terrible, like I was a bad son, so I'd immediately ask for forgiveness and fix the problem. To my surprise, she nodded, laughed knowingly, and said, "I try to break your heart, because when I die, you can't find me anymore." And there we have it, nicely summed up into one guilt trip-inducing quote. The truth had come out: she knew what she was doing all along. She was aware of the weight of those words and wasn't afraid to use them.

Turns out that *Cuando yo me muera* is part of a psychological battle. Our moms know exactly which buttons to push to make us step up to the plate if we're being difficult. They're trying to get a positive reaction out of us, even though the content of their message, death, is on the other side of the spectrum. As weird as this may sound, this phrase probably also is an inspirational tactic, very skillfully used by our mothers, or what I like to call motivation through manipulation. They know that when they pull the death card, the likelihood of getting us to do whatever they want increases threefold. It's the ultimate Jedi mind trick.

At the end of the day, the underlying lesson is really about not leaving for tomorrow what can be done today, about living a life without regrets, and about waking up, being present, and showing gratitude and appreciation for the life we have today because *cuando yo me muera* . . .

# #Education

O N  T H E  F I R S T  day of school, our homes are bustling with excitement. *"¡Despiértense!* You're going back to school!" our parents say, eagerly waking us up to get ready for our new year of education. One of them ushers us into the bathroom while the other prepares breakfast. We sleepily go through the motions, get dressed, and walk out of our rooms into flashing lights, as our mom takes practice paparazzi shots of the must-have first-day-of-school picture for everyone to see, an essential Hispanic tradition.

*"¡Wow, pero qué buen mozo! Esa belleza la sacaste de mí,"* exclaims your mom, gushing over your good looks and how you got them from her.

"Do we have to do this?" you say, naïvely hoping she will put away the camera.

*"Ay, mi niño, no seas tonto. Tú sabes que esto es tradición.*

*Échate un poquito pa' allá,"* she says, ignoring your complaint and making you move to the side so she can get a better shot. *"¡Pero, niño, sonríe!"* she adds, urging you to give her your best smile, and *snap, snap, snap,* the photo session is complete.

As you have breakfast, she quickly downloads the photos to her computer and picks her favorite one to post online for the world to see because nothing makes our parents prouder than showing off our successful education. The goal all Hispanic parents have is to see their children through elementary school, middle school, high school, and graduating from college with a degree in hand ready to conquer the world. Getting a solid education is so important in our community that it is practically engraved in our minds from the moment we come out of our mothers' wombs. Our parents take one look at us and already envision a lawyer, doctor, or CEO. That's why these first-day-of-school pictures are also so important. They form a record of each and every step we are taking to reach that venerated goal our parents have set for us—the first and foremost important goal of our young lives.

Once the perfect photo has been snapped and uploaded and you approach your mom to give her a kiss before leaving, she embraces you and says something along the lines of "You have to study hard to get good grades because you have to go to college," even if you're only six years old and just starting elementary school. *"Así que hazle caso a tu maestra, que yo sé que tú vas a ser un abogado o un doctor,"* she adds, asking you to listen to your teacher because there's a lawyer, doctor, and valedictorian in you. Some years, my mom would go all out and pull out the family camcorder. "Mami, please," I'd beg, "this is so embarrassing," but she'd continue to film me as I left the house and jumped into the car, waving goodbye with her free hand as if I were off to the airport on a yearlong trip. "*Pórtese bien.* Be good," she'd yell as the car pulled out of the driveway.

As I got older and went from elementary school to middle school and then high school, regardless of where we were living, the first-day-of-school photo tradition remained intact. What did evolve was the awareness of my surroundings. Middle school was when I started to understand what it meant to be Hispanic, what made us different from my American friends and their families, like how we greet each other, what we eat, the rules we must obey at home, and the expectations our parents have of us and our education. I also began to realize that when I hung out with my Hispanic friends at their homes, there was a common thread among all of us, regardless of what country we came from, and it felt more like home. It was an awakening of sorts, but it didn't stop me from making friends from all over the world.

I didn't want to confine myself to one group or one mindset, so when I hit my high school years in Central Florida, I relished the diversity and befriended classmates from different ethnic backgrounds, wanting to explore as many cultures as I could within my school days. I was pretty popular at school, got along with everyone, and loved to make people laugh. Since I wasn't allowed to sleep over at friends' houses and I wasn't a party guy, my main socializing happened between 8:30 a.m. and 3:30 p.m., and after school with my baseball teammates. The rest of the day was spent at my abuela's house or at home. I usually kept my head down and didn't get into too much trouble . . . usually.

When it came to schoolwork, I was pretty lazy and probably would've never managed to be the decent 3.2 GPA student I was had it not been for my fear of getting bad grades and dealing with the consequences at home. My sister was a scholar from the get-go, graduating as valedictorian and eventually getting her Ph.D. She was the model pupil, someone I always looked up to, and my parents knew they had nothing to worry about on that front, so all eyes fell on me (my brother is seven years younger than me, so his turn came later). My main strategy was to do just enough to get by so as not to incite my mom's fury. That meant pushing hard enough to remain slightly above a 3.0 GPA. This is something my American friends never completely understood. Most of them could get by at home with a C. "No, man, I can't get a C. I have to always aim for A's. Even a B could get me into some trouble," I'd say, trying to explain how it worked at my house. My friends would just stare at me somewhat bewildered, and then say something like, "My mom doesn't care that much. As long as I don't flunk out of a class, I'm good." Not my family. "Why are you so afraid of getting a C?" one of them would add. Where to begin?

Getting a C meant getting into serious trouble. It was grounds for a sit-down talk about how I could not under any circumstances neglect my education in this way, that a C was a disgrace to my parents and a disservice to my future. *"¿Tú sabes todo lo que nosotros sacrificamos para que tú te des el lujo de traer una C a la*

## Real-World Lessons

An important part of my education didn't just happen at school and at home, it happened in the Dominican Republic. While my parents told me that people back home didn't have it as easy as I did, that their educational opportunities didn't even come close to what I took for granted, they sent me there during the summers to see it for myself. They sent me back to my roots, to where I came from. I loved those summers because I had an awesome time, but I also learned to see the world from another perspective. My family in the Dominican Republic is incredibly selfless. Regardless of how much or how little they may have, they are willing to share it all with you. That's where I learned the real meaning of Hispanic generosity—you know, the people who will share the food off of their own plates so that neither of you goes hungry. Back home, they aren't focusing so much on what they don't have, but rather thanking God for what they do have. It's a lesson no school will ever teach you, but one that most Hispanics learn either by seeing it for themselves or through osmosis from their parents. Those of us who have had a decent upbringing can't forget that it wasn't always like that for our ancestors. We may roll our eyes when our parents go into their diatribes about all that had to happen for us to actually even get an education, but it's important to understand where they're coming from and where we come from so as to never lose sight of the roots that make us who we are today.

*casa?*" I started saying my prayers right then and there, because I knew some form of punishment would usually follow to get the point across. And a few times my mom added the dreaded statement, "That's it, I'm coming in," which was code for "I'm making an appointment with your guidance counselor," and I shuddered.

A meeting with the guidance counselor meant that my mom would drag me with her to his office to get to the bottom of my class slipups. It was excruciatingly embarrassing, pretty much like my "Parent Teacher Conference" video—where'd you think I got the inspiration? And she wouldn't stop until she had some answers and a clear way to fix such an unacceptable situation. "He's a good student, he just needs to apply himself," the counselor would say. My mom would listen quietly and carefully while I trembled in my seat beside her with each quick glance she shot at me.

Sometimes she would go so far as to explain my rebellious streak at home and how my parents worried I was hanging out with the wrong crowd at school, as if my guidance counselor could keep tabs on every student's choice in friends! But my mom didn't care. She and my dad were willing to go to extreme measures to keep me on the straight and narrow. My counselor would professionally guide the conversation back to my performance in school, explaining that one of my grades had dropped because I hadn't turned in a specific assignment. My heart skipped a beat. *Nooo, what is he doing? He's sending me straight to my funeral,* I thought as he continued to discuss areas where I could improve. Mami kept it together—mainly because she didn't want to cause a public scandal—and calmly reacted to this fact that she had been unaware of until now, while my mind kept racing. *I am in so much trouble. My dad is going to kill me when I get home.* The gut-wrenching fear that took hold of me with each second that ticked by in those meetings was almost worse than the *pela* I had to face later.

It wasn't just the dire consequences of getting a below-average grade that made my heart drop, it was the sheer disappointment on my parents' faces that absolutely did me in. Because there's nothing worse than disappointing our hardworking mothers and fathers. Even if we act like rebellious teenagers who don't care, it is really ripping us apart inside, and our parents rip us to even further shreds. "What did we do to you to deserve this?" That's the clincher. Ultimately, they feel that it's their fault, that they have failed us as parents, and that now all is lost in the world. I know, a little dramatic, but they really just want the best for us. The only solution is to step up to the plate and prove them wrong by getting those grades up and reaching the holy grail of graduation.

Despite my couple of C's and rebellious streak, I did graduate. I wasn't valedictorian, but I kept my GPA above 3.0 and had my parents in the audience bawling when I stood up to get my diploma. Now what? Well, college, of course. Hispanic families will not have it any other way.

I grew up dreaming of doing something in the world of sports. As an incredibly passionate sports fan—my artistic name is inspired by my all-time favorite basketball player, LeBron

James—but not such a great player, I leaned toward becoming a sports agent or sports therapist, and finally decided to pursue a degree in marketing with the idea of later diving into the world of sports marketing. Meanwhile, my sister was off studying abroad and getting her degree at the prestigious Rollins College in Florida, doing outstandingly well as always in all her educational endeavors. I love her and couldn't be more proud of her, but as much as I admired and respected her, that bar was set way too high for me! My parents assumed I would follow in her footsteps, so when I enrolled in a community college and then decided to call it quits, I immediately became the black sheep of the family. They were shocked and disappointed beyond belief. Wow, how I wished I was back in high school, living the simple life, rather than out on my own having to deal with the laundry list of responsibilities of the real world and my parents' disillusionment as the cherry on top of it all.

Going against the grain, making our own future, walking off the beaten path are things our traditional Hispanic parents do not take lightly. Despite how thrilling and invigorating following our calling may be to us, our parents see this as an unstable journey that might not always put food on the table, which is the polar opposite of what they envisioned when they came to the United States.

What they sometimes don't realize is that here, not only do we have the chance for a solid education but we are also exposed to the realm of possibilities this country has to offer, and some of us decide to take a leap of faith and follow our own dreams. In my case, this meant finishing my associate's degree and then focusing on my full-time job with the hope of climbing the corporate ladder the old-school way, from entry level to manager, to wherever else that might take me. This was before social media was even on my radar as a career, so my decisions also meant dealing with countless lectures in my young adult life: "What do you mean, community college and that's it?" "You have to get your life together." "You won't go anywhere without a four-year college degree."

Those times were difficult because I knew how much my parents cared about me, how much they wanted to see me complete a bachelor's degree. The last thing I wanted to do was let them down, but I also knew in my heart that I had to follow my gut. I tried to explain this to my parents—I've always had a passion for learning, but not so much for school—but it was like a slap in the face to them. The truth is I was never really good at sitting still in a classroom, listening attentively to the teacher, and absorbing the information received. Unlike my sister and some of my cousins, who were all bookworms, I was easily distracted and found it hard to learn that way. Mami didn't get it. She was worried sick about my choice, was sad that I wasn't taking advantage of the opportunities she and my dad didn't have when they were my age, but she also knew it was time to let me fly from the nest and make my own decisions, even if she did think I was throwing my life away.

The last thing she wanted was for me to face the tough road she and my dad had had to face: the double shifts, the two jobs, the inability to meet mortgage payments, the works. That's why our parents will always cheer us on at school events, keep a close watch over our grades, reach out to the guidance counselor to help set us straight. That's why they cry tears of joy when we walk across the stage and receive our diplomas, because all they want is the absolute best for their children. Sometimes they just have to have a little faith in our own callings, even if they are somewhat unconventional. You never know until you try!

# #LifeLessonsAreEverywhere

**E**VERY MOMENT IS a teachable moment in the Hispanic community. Life lessons are everywhere we turn. With sayings, *refranes*, and proverbs coming at us from every elder member in our family, it is hard to escape them. Some are new lessons that arrive in the heat of the moment, while others have been passed down from generation to generation, like the classic *Al mal tiempo, buena cara,* which is similar to *Put on a brave face.* Old or new, our parents and grandparents practically talk in lessons. You could be holding an incredibly light conversation about the weather and how when it's cold you feel like staying in bed a little while longer, and then suddenly be hit with *Al que madruga Dios lo ayuda,* and a lecture on how the early bird gets the worm.

A classic scenario of an impromptu life lesson at my house was when I was teenager and I'd ask my parents for a few dollars to fill up the tank with gas. They would give me the money, but not without first teaching me a life lesson on how saving is important.

"Where's your money going? I see you buying clothes and sneakers, but do you have a savings account?" my dad would instantly reply, as he pulled out his wallet from his back pocket.

"Dad, I just asked you for a few bucks for gas," I'd say, annoyed.

*"Pero, hijo, ¿qué hiciste con el dinero que te di la semana pasada? Chico, tú tienes que aprender a manejar mejor tu dinero si no quieres quedarte pelao."* He'd keep going until he made sure I understood the value of the five dollars he was handing over to me and how important comprehending and adopting the concept of saving would be for my future.

He was right, but at the time I thought it was all nonsense. Growing up, I never really needed anything. We were like most middle-class families, with presents on birthdays and a delicious spread on the table for dinner. I never knew that many times we were actually living paycheck to paycheck, and that my parents had moments of hardship when they were stretching themselves thin to provide us with a solid upbringing and education, because they never burdened us with their adult problems. However, they were always heavy on the lessons, making sure we understood the value of a dollar so we would become aware at an early age of just how much work was required to earn that money and how easy it was to spend it.

So, if any of us kids approached my dad before Christmas asking for the latest iPhone, we'd get a lesson on how when he was a child he would've never even dared asked his father for such an expensive gift. "I just accepted whatever I received from my parents. *A caballo regalao no se le mira el colmillo,*" he'd say, and then close by pulling out his ancient flip phone. "*Esto sirve para hacer llamadas.* I don't understand why you need something so fancy to make a few phone calls." It was useless to try to explain any further. He was right, none of us really *needed* the latest iPhone, but as kids growing up in the United States, we found it hard not to compare ourselves to our classmates and not want what they had—it's human nature. And sometimes, if we were lucky and our parents were in a good place and could afford such luxuries, they'd get us the gifts of our choosing, but not without first making sure we didn't lose sight of the value of such a gift and what it took to acquire it. By doing so, although we would've loved to be spared the speech, they were teaching us that hard work and discipline pay off in the long run.

Even something as basic as sitting down at the dinner table came with a lesson. If our parents happened to notice that we still had food on our plates and had no intention of finishing it, they'd start out with the classic "*Termina la comida que si no, no te paras hasta que termines de comer.*" We've all heard that one before, and sometimes we took it as an empty threat, but most of the time they drilled the point further.

"*Eso es un pecado. Tú tienes que acabar esa comida.*"

"But, Mami, I'm fuuull . . ."

"*En esta casa no se desperdicia la comida,*" final answer.

Throwing away good food was out of the question, because we don't let anything go to waste. So if your eye was bigger than your stomach and you helped yourself to a larger serving than you could finish, tough luck. Not finishing our entire meal was disrespectful not only to the person who toiled in the kitchen after a long day's work, but also to those who could use an extra helping of food before bed. As if stuffing our faces with every last grain of rice from our plate would make food magically appear on someone else's.

I had to finish the food on my plate to show appreciation and remember that others didn't have this luxury. I had to finish my homework before turning on the TV to learn discipline. I had to help tidy up to learn teamwork. I had to pray and give thanks before going to bed to learn to always thank God for every blessing we are granted. No matter what was going on, no matter how much my parents were struggling or thriving, those house rules were ever-present and meant to be respected and followed no matter what. *En la casa hispana, las reglas se mantienen.* To this day, and I know many of you are going to relate, I still feel guilty if I leave food on my plate.

Nothing that our parents or grandparents ever do is in vain, no matter how strange we might find it. All of their lessons are part of their motivational plan to turn us into decent, hard-working, and successful individuals. Like that one time I was home alone and decided to grab a beer from the fridge. I was a teenager, I'd never had a beer before, and curiosity got the best of me. It wasn't like I was downing a six-pack. I just opened one beer bottle, took a few swigs, and quickly put it back before my parents got home. Dumb move. Later that evening, when my mom opened the refrigerator door, she immediately noticed the all too visible opened and half-drunk bottle mockingly staring at her.

"Who opened this beer?" she said, knowing that my dad would never have left a half-empty bottle in the fridge.

"I did. I opened it," I said, immediately fessing up and trying to explain I had just taken a few sips out of curiosity, but it was like I had confessed that I had been drinking morning, noon, and night for the past year.

Curiosity most definitely killed the cat that day—I was in for one of the lectures of my life. My parents immediately sat me down and began by explaining how drugs and alcohol could hinder my coherence and affect my life in the short and long terms. How they could deter me from any and all types of happiness, health, and success, and how I had to stay away from drugs and alcohol at all costs if I wanted to lead a good life. Talk about going overboard! I only wanted to have a sip of beer and see what the rest of my family was drinking at our gatherings. I was an intrigued teenager, I wasn't trying to get drunk or turn into a raging alcoholic, but my mom and dad immediately feared the worst. The whole diatribe felt more like an intervention than a simple "You're too young to be drinking anything but juice, water, and soda. Just wait a few more years." And this was only the first of many "interventions" to come.

Another time, I had just finished messing around with friends with a bag of *petardos*—those party snaps that you throw on the ground for a quick little firecracker noise effect—and had left the empty bag on the nightstand in my room. I honestly didn't even think twice about it, but now I realize that if you looked at it out of context, just sitting on the nightstand, you could easily have mistaken it for a weed bag. Lord have mercy! It never crossed my mind until that day when my dad walked in and his heart stopped at the horror. He slowly picked up the bag, turned to me, and said in a serious, upset, and slightly fearful voice, "What is this?" I was about to reply, but he kept going. "Have you been smoking weed? Who are you hanging out with? *What's going on?*" I tried to calm him down and explain that it was just an empty bag of *petardos,* but he wasn't having it. If only one measly little party snap had been left inside the bag, that would've been my saving grace. No such luck. He dove into a lecture on how drugs could affect my brain and my life, how I had to be careful who I hung out with, how I should choose my friends wisely to avoid going down this road to nowhere.

As annoying as it may have been back then—and believe me, I rolled my eyes as much as the next kid at these lectures—it all came from a deep love for me and a profound fear that I would take the wrong path and turn my future into a shambles. As long as I was under their roof, abiding by their rules, my parents had a sense of control, but they knew the minute I walked out the door, there was nothing they could really do. Therefore, regardless of how well behaved I was, if they saw any inkling that I might be around drugs or alcohol, be it because I was hanging out with the wrong crowd (which wasn't the case) or talking back to them with smart-ass comebacks (which sometimes was the case), that's all they needed to hit me with the drug talk, the alcohol talk, the warnings of how both substances could ruin my life, as if I were already some sort of hardened criminal.

So, yes, sometimes it felt like I was always being accused of crimes I didn't commit—guilty until proven innocent—but now I know that my parents were really just looking out for me, hoping to stuff my mind with as many lessons as possible before I flew the nest and they could no longer protect me. There is an enormous amount of value in each and every one of those lessons. The advice our elders give us truly holds a tremendous amount of weight; it's worth perking up and listening to these hidden gems of wisdom, because they will come in handy one day.

# #ReduceReuseRecycle

**I**T'S A WEEKDAY morning like any other. Your parents have left for work early and you're getting ready for school. A slice of bread is on your plate and all you need is some butter and jam. You open the fridge, reach for the Country Crock container, put it on the counter, and open it, knife ready in your right hand to dig in, when suddenly you smell . . . garlic. *What?* You take a peek into the container and find that instead of butter there's leftover *sofrito*. Frantically, you go back to the fridge and start opening other containers, realizing that none of their labels match their contents. That's when you know . . . you're not in Kansas anymore. Welcome to recycling the Hispanic way, where nothing is thrown away and every single thing we have is given a new lease on life, no questions asked.

Let's start with the basics. When you leave a room, always turn the light off, especially if you don't want to get hit with the talk about running up the already high electricity bill and how you're not the one breaking your back to make the money to pay it. So just turn the light off and save yourself some time. Plus, by doing so, you are unintentionally saving energy, which is great for the environment, so it's a win-win situation. I learned the hard way. My issue wasn't forgetting to turn the lights off, it was falling asleep with the TV on. Every time it happened, I'd get woken up by my mom's or dad's pissed-off yell, "You want to sleep with the TV on? Fine. *Cuando llegue la luz, itú la vas a pagar!*" And while you're at it, keep an eye on the water. Whenever I got carried away singing in the shower for a few minutes too long, I'd get several angry knocks at the door together with a *"Tú no pagas el agua. Avanza, sal de ahí."* And sometimes one of my parents would add, "You're wasting all the hot water, *niño!*" Wait, but we have running hot water. *"Sí, ¿pero qué tú crees?* It still costs money to heat it." And this is just the tip of the iceberg.

Now that the utilities are covered, let's move to the staples: shampoo, dish soap, and toothpaste. Do you know what they all have in common? They're never as empty as they seem. If I happened to call out to my mom from the shower saying we'd run out of shampoo, she'd open the door and stop cold at the sight of the bottle. *"Tú estás loco? ¿No ves que le queda un montón?"* I'd stare back puzzled. "What do you mean, there's still a lot left? Mami, can't you see it's empty?" With an annoyed look, she'd grab the bottle from my hand, disappear, and return with a "new" one, end of discussion. I always noticed it was a bit diluted, but knew better than to question her. As usual, she had pulled the old "fill the bottle with water and shake it like a maraca" trick, which I have seen her do so often with dish soap too. If there's a line of soap at the bottom of the bottle, water will be added to it, done deal. Toothpaste can also be deceiving. Water won't help in this case, but a pair of scissors will. When you think you've squeezed every last drop out, cut the tube, dig your toothbrush into it, and get to brushing. You'll find there's still enough to go around for at least another day or two, or so say our moms.

Next up, expiration dates. I'll admit, I'm much more Americanized when it comes to these dates. If something is past its date, I will not think twice about throwing it out. But not my parents. If they saw me throwing out a carton of milk, they'd stop me in my tracks, grab the carton, ignore the date, and simply open it up and take a whiff.

"*No, chico, esto está bueno todavía*," they'd say, and back in the fridge it went.

"Are you serious? This is expired! There's a date on it for a reason. I'm not drinking that milk," I'd reply, kind of grossed out that they'd decided to keep the milk because it *smelled* okay.

"*¿Y qué?* You want me to throw this away? *Yo pagué por esto.* We gotta drink it."

That's right, their sense of smell is more powerful than the FDA's expiration date. Moreover, they already paid for it, and nothing goes to waste. So do yourself a favor and forget about those pesky expiration dates, because they mean nothing in a Hispanic home. If it smells good, looks good, and tastes good, then it's fine. "*Cómetelo.*"

From day one, our parents make sure we appreciate what we have, that we're grateful, knowing nothing comes easy and nothing is free, so waste is out of the question. *El desperdicio es una falta de respeto.* Be it the shampoo, the food on your plate, or the rickety TV, everything we have is precious, and we are taught to use the last drop, eat the last morsel, and fix what's broken before even considering throwing something away. Sending our stuff to the trash, have you lost your mind? That is always and forever the absolute last resort, and only because the object in question has shattered into a million useless pieces. If not, there's always a handyman or a relative who will fix it or an uncle who can take it off our hands or a seamstress who can turn it into something else. And "it" can be anything from an old piece of furniture to a TV or even a car.

I approached my dad about the latter once. To this day, he still refuses to give up our old minivan, even though my parents have a brand-new car. I've tried all the angles and have repeatedly calmly suggested that it may be time to let this one go, but all I get in reply is "No, we can still do things with this. *Si alguien se tiene que mudar o si necesitamos llevar mucha gente para alguna parte . . .*" And with that, the run-down minivan remains in the garage with oil puddling beneath it, literally breaking down before our eyes . . . just in case someone needs help moving one day or we have to take a lot of people somewhere. The lack of specificity kills me. And if that day ever comes, I wonder whether the thing would even make it to its destination. But there's no sense in arguing; better luck next time.

That same garage is filled with useless stuff my mom continues to hoard thinking that one of those items may come in handy for somebody one day too. Again, what item, who needs it, and when? No answers. Totally vague. All I get from her is *"Eso sirve todavía"* or *"Eso se puede usar en el futuro."* And if you're thinking this has to do with having grown up poor, I'm sorry to burst your bubble. It goes beyond economic status. We were never below the poverty line, but that didn't stop my family from stashing ketchup packs and extra napkins in Mami's purse at restaurants. "Throw them away? No, no, save them. We can use them later." Splenda is a highly valued commodity too. One minute it's on the table, the next minute it is wiped clean. I found this sooo embarrassing when I was a kid, but as the years passed, I got used to it. A leopard doesn't change its spots, so we either accept them or die trying.

In all the moves we've made, I don't ever recall placing old furniture in front of the house and driving away. There was always someone ready and able to take whatever we no longer needed off our hands. We'd never throw away good furniture. We just don't do that. So when we first moved to the United States, it was a huge culture shock for us all to see furniture on the sidewalk with TAKE WHAT YOU WANT or FREE signs next to it. Sometimes my mom would say, *"Eso se ve bueno,"* and next thing I knew we had a new used piece of furniture in our living room. My mom loves a good garage sale. Furniture, clothes, you name it, *"Esto lo lavo y queda como nuevo."* It just takes one wash to turn an old piece of clothing into a new stylish outfit.

As much as we hoard, save, and reuse, sometimes we have no choice but to accept that our stuff has run its course and it is time to give it up. Note that I didn't say "throw it away." Nope. Give up. Give away. To a cousin, an aunt, an uncle, a friend—it doesn't matter, so long as we find it a new home.

The clear sign that one of these major giveaways was about to take place was when my mom pulled out the boxes. She would buy these big brown cardboard moving boxes, pack them up with all the stuff we no longer used or needed, and ship them off to the Dominican Republic. Anytime I saw them lying around, I thought, *Oh, no, here we go again,* and I'd rush to my room to do a quick count of the stuff I still wanted to keep and stash it away to protect it from the magical disappearing act that would soon take place. Not giving anything away was unacceptable, so once I had safeguarded my valuables, I'd sweep the room again and choose the stuff that I could fathom parting with to help fill those brown boxes. I didn't realize it at the time, but this tortuous biannual event actually taught me to truly put thought into what I use and don't use, and what could be useful to someone else—a lesson I still hold close to my heart.

My mom helped me reorganize my closet recently, and man, did she have a field day. There's a whole bunch of stuff that I don't wear, and she knows it, so she turned to me with a twinkle in her eye.

"What are you going to do with this?" she asked, coyly.

"What do you mean, 'What am I going to do with this?' These are my clothes; this is my closet."

"Well, you don't wear this stuff. We can send this to your cousins in the Dominican Republic."

I grew up in a middle-class family. However, the last thing my parents wanted was for my siblings and me to lose sight of the value of what we had, where we came from, and what other people must do to survive. To drive the point home, they didn't just give us speeches, they sent us on summer vacations to the Dominican Republic with my grandparents, so that we could catch a glimpse of a different life with our own eyes.

I had a ball. It was the best break ever, being surrounded by cousins to play with and eating foods that are still among my top favorites to this day. It also helped me see my mom's big-box giveaways from another perspective and finally get it. One day—actually this happened more than once—one of my cousins walked into my abuela's house and I couldn't stop staring at his chest, thinking, *Wait a minute, I have a shirt just like that,* only to realize that *was* my shirt, the one I thought I had misplaced back home. It had obviously gotten caught in my mom's last spring-cleaning sweep of our house. When I asked my mom about this, complaining because it was one of my favorite shirts, she replied, somewhat annoyed, "Well, you never wore it anymore, so it didn't seem like you loved it that much." Sentimental value will not cut it when there are others who can make use of your stuff, especially if you're a kid.

Another time, I was hanging out with one of my cousins in his room when something from his bed caught my eye. *"¡Oh, yo tengo unas sábanas igualitas a estas!"* I exclaimed, excited to see we had the same sheets. He just gave me a quick nod, stared back at me in silence, then changed the subject. Only later did I realize that those actually *were* my old sheets. After a few of these incidents, I finally understood where most of our give-aways and hand-me-downs ended up.

As I got a little older, I started to become aware of some of the comforts we took for granted back home. Some relatives in the Dominican Republic didn't have AC; I'm talking no window unit, nothing. Others had gravel or sand instead of tiled floor, some didn't have a roof over their heads, and running hot water was a luxury. I didn't really pay attention to these differences when I was a child. I thought it was normal to go to the Dominican Republic and take quick cold showers and sleep under a mosquito net because the windows had no glass or screens. I really didn't care either, because I always had so much fun with my cousins. But as I got older, these differences became more apparent and put into perspective how good we really had it back home. I'm glad I got to see this as a kid, because it made an enormous impact on how I view the world today.

Now I'm the one setting aside clothes and other stuff I no longer want or need and sending it to my relatives, who will give these things new life. Now I understand the value of letting go of things that are just sitting in my closet collecting dust. And even though I have still not quite wrapped my head around the whole matter of filling what I think are empty bottles with water to make use of the line of soap or shampoo left at the bottom or cutting toothpaste tubes to scoop out the last bit of paste, I understand where it's coming from. We don't reduce, reuse, and recycle to save the environment (although it's greatly benefited by our customs), we do these things because, no matter how much or how little we may have, we are taught to never take it for granted and to share with others what we do not need, because our junk could be someone else's treasure.

# #SuperstitionsPremonitionsandHomeRemedies

I F YOU'RE HISPANIC, you have no doubt been taught to respect certain superstitions, take heed of premonitions, and abide by specific home remedies. Like me, you may not believe in some of these myths and cure-all concoctions, but we're not about to tempt fate by not following them. Even though our logical minds may realize some of this stuff doesn't make sense, we will still not open an umbrella inside the house or walk underneath a ladder, to avoid bad luck. Better to be safe than sorry.

## Superstitions

When we toast, we must always make eye contact, because who wants to risk being hit with seven years of bad sex? If someone asks us to pass the salt, rather than hand it to them, we place it on the table next to them to avoid getting into a fight. When our ears ring, someone is talking about us. And, ladies, do not for any reason place your purse on the floor. I learned this last one from my mom. Every time someone set a purse on the floor, she would go crazy. *"¡Niña, levanta esa cartera de ahí que si no te llega el dinero!"* she'd say, grabbing the bag like she was an outfielder trying to catch a fly ball to avoid the next home run. I used to be astounded by this intense reaction, but it's contagious. I respect and follow the superstitions I grew up with even if I don't believe them wholeheartedly . . . and I even have some that I do think are true. When my right hand itches, I get super excited because I know that means I'll be receiving money soon. Does this make sense? No. But I'm Hispanic. Most of the stuff discussed in this essay doesn't make sense to the uninformed, but it's a no-brainer to us.

*Mal de ojo*, the evil eye, is another good example. Getting cast with a *mal de ojo* is one of our greatest fears, especially when it comes to our kids, because it brings bad luck and can even inflict injury. The worst part? You likely won't even know when you've been cursed. That's why, when you have a string of bad luck or when you're continually getting sick, we will always mention *mal de ojo* as the possible culprit. Our elders have ways of diagnosing this unfortunate ailment. Once it is confirmed, you must get rid of it ASAP and then protect yourself from future spells. The remedies can range from a prayer and a *limpieza* to a full-blown Mass and the sprinkling of holy water to ward off the evil spirit that has got you in that rut. Once you are cured, there are bracelets, necklaces, and candles you can use to keep the *mal de ojo* from striking again. The basic goal is to shake off the negative energy that has you spinning in a loop of misfortune and get on with your life.

Our families start us off on these superstitious rules and beliefs at a young age, with the mythical monster we all grew up fearing as kids: El Cuco. That name has sent a chill down the spines of countless Hispanic children—it is the Freddy Krueger of our childhood. Hearing *"El Cuco te va a agarrar"* put the fear of God in us and made us obey whatever our parents were telling us to do. As a kid, I never even dared to go into our backyard at night because I thought El Cuco was patiently waiting in the bushes, ready to pounce on me as soon as I stepped out into the darkness. The truth is none of us really knows what El Cuco looks like; it's open to our imaginations. I saw it as a hairy creature with horns and saliva drooling between its sharp teeth. It's basically the most terrifying thing you can drum up in those years when monsters and demons are as real as your pounding heartbeat. And it's the perfect decoy for parents to get their children to do what they want, like behave or go to sleep when we're disturbing the peace. And it works every time until the end of its life span, which is usually when we enter our preteen years and it is replaced with our belief in the power of our dreams.

## Dreams as Premonitions

In the Hispanic community, there is a firmly held belief that dreams, whether good or bad, are not meant to be ignored. They are messages or premonitions that serve a distinct purpose: to project what will happen in our future or that of people we know. When we go to sleep, we enter another world, where we work out our problems or connect with God to communicate on a deeper level. Every scene that unfolds in this dream world carries meaning in the real world too.

Some people may believe that dreams are intimate, that these messages are meant to be kept to yourself, but not us. Hispanics love to share our dreams and get to the bottom of what our subconscious or God is trying to tell us. Look, I'll be honest, I can't remember any of my dreams, but I have mad respect for them, and as hard as interpreting dreams as premonitions may be to understand, I believe they serve a purpose. Don't worry if you're like me and you don't remember your dreams or don't know how to read them. There's a mom or an abuela for that.

In my case, it's my mom. She has the gift of interpreting all the signs hiding in our dreams. My cousin Arisel many times calls my mom just to talk about her dreams. The point is to figure out not only what they mean, but also how to use their messages to our advantage, to be extra-cautious in case something bad may be heading our way. It's not always doom and gloom, though. We stay tuned for signs of a favorable future outcome too.

When my cousin calls, my mom will go all in and follow a line of questioning that will help her further decipher the images she is describing. For example, if Arisel says someone is at the door, then my mom needs to know if she can identify the person, if he or she is holding the door, if the person is inside, or outside trying to come in. If Arisel mentions water, then my mom needs to know if it's a pond, an ocean, or a river, if it's moving or still, and so forth. Every detail counts, because it could affect the meaning of the entire dream.

I don't usually participate in these conversations since I don't remember my dreams, but I sit by and listen in awe at my mom's knowledge. I find it crazy and fascinating. Where did she get all of this information? How does she remember so many symbols and meanings? How is she able to put two and two together and turn a random dream into a clear message, and usually get it right? Well, it's not through Google. I mean, sure, she'll look some stuff up if needed, but most of it is passed on from generation to generation, through osmosis, as a form of spoken wisdom.

As I mentioned before, we have no qualms about sharing our dreams during a family lunch, while sipping a *cafecito,* on the phone, or at the dinner table. All we want is to get to the bottom of the premonition so we can be prepared for what's to come or call whoever popped up in those images just to make sure that person is okay. When someone says to us, *"Tuve un sueño contigo,"* our bodies tense up because we know the dream that person had could carry an equally happy or ominous premonition. We might be afraid of what we may be told, but curiosity always gets the best of us in the end.

My mom takes dream interpretation to another level. If she happens to wake up in the middle of a dream and leaves it unresolved, she will turn around, fall back asleep, and pick up where she left off in order to fix the issue before starting her day. Yes, you read right! She wills herself back to sleep to sort it all out, then wakes up again, satisfied with the results. Once awake, she turns to my dad to share her dream with him (you should never keep a dream to yourself!), and then asks him about his own to help him sort through the meaning of the jumbled images in his mind if he has any to recall. It's part of their morning ritual.

A little more than a year ago, my mom woke up from a specific dream on the day she was scheduled for minor surgery, and she knew that what she saw while she was asleep was warning her that she would face complications. Instead of prepping for an operation that was supposed to be a same-day thing, she packed a small bag, and sure enough, a one-hour procedure turned into an eight-hour overnight ordeal. She was fine in the end, but just as her dream had predicted, her doctors faced a few unexpected roadblocks along the way.

Now I can see my fiancée, Camila, developing this ability to read between the lines of her dreams. When we wake up, we'll talk about what she dreamed and analyze it until she can figure out how to interpret the hidden message. My role is more of a listener fascinated by her thought process and how she is slowly becoming better and quicker at making sense of the unthinkable. We Hispanics are constantly in search of the significance behind what we dream and what happens to us, hoping to find insight to help guide us toward the best path in our lives . . . or at least the one that's not going to kill us before our time!

## Classic Home Remedies

*"¡Qué doctor ni doctor! ¡Si yo estoy bien! Me hago un tecito con un chin de limón y quedo como nueva."* That's right, a tea and a

dash of lemon is all we need to cure many of our common ailments. Doctors are highly respected in the Hispanic community. If you are a doctor, you are our hero, curing people and saving lives, but we will do everything in our power to avoid visiting you. There is absolutely no way we are going to drag any of our Hispanic relatives to the doctor unless they are practically on their deathbeds. It's just a fact, so don't fight it. We will first try our long list of home remedies and any other potions we can drum up before caving to the pressure and calling to make a doctor's appointment. As much as we admire the medical professionals of the world, we are prone to self-diagnosing first and then self-medicating. If our parents think we're running a fever, they don't pull out a thermometer, they use the backs of their hands or place their cheeks to our foreheads. And if we're burning up, they'll say, *"Estás hirviendo, eso es que tienes fiebre,"* with all the confidence in the world that they will be able to get rid of that pesky fever their own way.

Hey, I'm a believer. Some of this stuff has worked on me. How? Why? No idea. But I'm not going to question it. There's a certain faith we learn to have in these home remedies that goes beyond science. We trust them. We know our parents want us to feel better, so we trust that they will find the necessary cure. When I feel sick and I'm around my parents, I instantly see the light at the end of the flu-infested tunnel. They know me better than anyone and give me what I need to get back on my two feet. Whatever it is, I will accept it. They are so incredibly resourceful, they are like my very own live WebMD.

You know what I'm talking about. If your mom comes into

your room with an onion and honey tea and tells you that drinking it will cure your fever, you drink it, regardless of how nasty that concoction might taste. In our community, there is a tea for every ailment; it's our first resort when we're feeling under the weather. Stomach problems? Out comes the *té de manzanilla,* or chamomile tea. Sore throat? Sage tea or a classic lemon, honey, and hot water combo. Want to lose weight? There's a tea for that. Need to calm your anxiety? There's a tea for that. Whatever you need cured, just reach out to your mom, tías, or abuelas and they'll set you straight with a specific tea.

Another go-to remedy is all forms of soup. The *sancocho,* a hearty vegetable and meat soup, can cure everything from a cold to a hangover. An onion, garlic, and ginger soup is your flu's worst nightmare. And the *sopa de pollo,* or chicken soup, is the universal medicine for any type of upper-respiratory ailment. I know there are countless recipes and variations from country to country, so when in doubt, don't Google it, just call up your relatives. They are your very own personally tailored search engine. The older they are, the better they remember each remedy. And if they can't figure it out, they will call another relative for their list of recipes. There is a collective knowledge saved in our community's mind that goes far beyond the reaches of any online search engine, so don't be afraid to tap into this priceless resource. In any case, don't worry, because as soon as news of your ailment hits the family grapevine, you will be getting calls from tías and abuelas chiming in with their perfect cures. Each one will share her own special recipe, her secret ingredient, and how to use it to work magic on your weak body. I don't know if it is

> ### ¡Ay Dios mío, déjame buscar el mentol!
>
> While your mom or abuela is brewing the specific tea to cure your illness, the other one is heading to the medicine cabinet to grab the be-all and end-all of Hispanic home remedies: Vicks VapoRub (a.k.a. Vicks or *el vivaporú*). Ever since I can remember, Vicks magically has appeared on my nightstand like an angel watching over me when I feel under the weather. When I was a kid, I'd crawl into bed to sleep off my flu and suddenly be jolted awake by the smell of menthol and a cold sensation on my chest. *"Ay, Mami, ¡no me vengas a bañar con esa vaina, por favor!"* I'd plead, asking my mom to spare me the Vicks bath, but it was like talking to a wall. Vicks VapoRub is our foolproof, cure-all holy grail of remedies. If you have a cold, put Vicks under your nose; if you have a cough, put it on your chest; if you have a headache, put it on your temples; if you have a broken heart, put it on your heart. If Vicks can't cure you, then you're in serious trouble.

mind over body or what, but whatever home remedy I am given usually does the trick, so I'm a believer through and through.

There is an inherent resilient spirit in Hispanics that comes from this faith that we are born into. Faith in God, faith in the meaning of life, faith in our dreams as premonitions, faith in our home remedies. No matter how tough it may get, we believe that there are no bad breaks and no meaningless events in our lives because God has a plan for all of us. Everything happens for a reason. Our wins and losses, our happiness and sorrows, they all hold a deeper meaning and lesson, and we will not rest until we know what this is. Even when it feels like the cards are stacked against us, we believe that only means better times are coming. This meaning and purpose in life make us a very optimistic and strong community. No matter how far or how hard we fall, no matter what may ail us, we will always get up, drink that special tea or whatever remedy is prescribed to us by our relatives, dust ourselves off, and keep going. We have faith that something better is just around the corner and are not afraid to rely on a little superstition, premonition, or remedy to cure us and guide us down the right path.

# #MusicIsInOurDNA

CRUISING DOWN the street, you pull up to a stoplight and brake, in your own little world, when suddenly the laundry list of thoughts scrolling through your mind is infiltrated by a melody. Puzzled, you look at your radio—it's off. Your head turns right, nothing. You glance left and do a double take. Sitting in the car next to you is a guy with his windows rolled down, blasting salsa, and singing at the top of his lungs. You catch his eye, and he glances back at you with a wide smile and yells out, *"¡Weeepaaaaaa!"* His hands suddenly fly up to his face and start playing air trumpet to mirror the tune's solo, while his body is swaying back and forth to the contagious rhythm of the music. All he wants to do is share the hot beats, heartfelt lyrics, and pure joy inspired by those songs with you and the world.

The guy in the car next to you—that's pretty much me! I

cannot drive without blasting music. I don't only need to hear it, I need to feel it, become one with it, whether it's a merengue, a classic seventies salsa tune, or a passionate ballad. I love music so much I don't want to just keep it to myself, I want to share it with my fellow drivers, share the song's joy, pain, and excitement. I can't help myself, it's in my blood, it's in our DNA. Haven't you seen all the viral videos of Hispanic babies jiggling left and right to the rhythm of their parents' favorite tunes? Everywhere we go, everything we do, is accompanied by music.

Our parents start us out young. As soon as we take our first steps, we're also learning our first merengue, bachata, or salsa moves. *"Báilale a tu tía pa' que te vea,"* our parents say as they urge us to show our tías our toddler moves. Soon enough, the music seeps into our ears, our diaper-clad baby hips start swinging back and forth, and we receive an instant standing ovation. *"¡Qué ritmo! Eso lo heredó de Mami."* With that type of encouragement, how are we not going to get into music?

I grew up listening to my dad's old-school seventies and eighties salsa albums. He had them on all the time. I heard Héctor Lavoe's *"Periódico de ayer,"* Frankie Ruiz's *"La cura,"* and Tito Rojas's *"Siempre seré"* so much that eventually they seeped into my own list of favorite tunes and became the classics I love to blast too. Music is playing morning, noon, and night in Hispanic homes, so you can't help but tune in to what your parents or siblings are listening to; it becomes part of your memories, your history, and your life. When my dad wasn't playing his tunes, my mom would be playing hers. Songs like La India's *"Ese hombre"* or *"Mi mayor venganza"* and Jerry Rivera's *"Amores como el nuestro"* would wake me on the weekends and let me know that my mom was already up and cleaning the house. I'd walk into the kitchen and find her washing the dishes and humming the song on the stereo, and when it got real good, we'd just break into a dance.

Like most Hispanics, I've been dancing since I was a kid. I grew up dancing with my mom, and I still do it to this day. We love it so much our faces light up and we'll find any excuse to start moving to the rhythm of a song, as some of our videos together can attest. Come on, are you really going to stand there and tell me you've never been overcome by the need to dance in your car, at a restaurant or bar, or at the supermarket when one of your jams starts playing on the radio? Suddenly, one foot starts tapping out the beat while you hum the chorus, and your body discreetly sways to the right and to the left. You can't help it. It's your muscle memory kicking into high gear. Music just gets us going.

No matter what we're doing, music will be playing in our lives like our very own personal soundtracks. I was just cleaning out my closet the other day while singing along to salsa tracks. If my mom is cooking, she has to have some music going to inspire her, and that will inevitably lead her to tapping the wooden spoon against the pot as if it were *timbales* and she was Tito Puente. And you know what happens when there's a broom in my hand . . . I channel my abuela and start stepping and turning as if I were dancing with JLo herself. Hispanics don't believe in background music. If we're going to play something, we're going to play it loud, so we can sing it loud, and dance like there's no tomorrow, even while doing house chores.

The other place I love to pump my music is in the shower. As soon as that bathroom door closes, the room becomes my stage. I turn up the music, grab a toothbrush, hairbrush, loofah, or whatever is within my reach, and start singing passionately into it as if that was the mic and I was performing in a stadium for fifty thousand people. The bathroom is also the ideal spot to perfect our dance moves. Are you really going to tell me you've never done this? Not even once? With that huge mirror perfectly reflecting every step, arm movement, and turn, it's impossible to look away. It's so entrancing that if someone happens to walk in mid-performance, it's like a bucket of ice-cold water. We freeze in place, then scurry around trying to act all normal, and get annoyed at the intruder for not letting us shower in peace, though we're as dry as bones and have not even stepped into the shower stall yet.

I have a few videos showcasing this shower scenario because I know it all too well. I've been doing this for years at home; the moment takes over and I am completely committed to it. So much so that when I was a kid, oftentimes I'd hear my parents yelling at me from the living room, *"¡Baja la voz, que estás gritando!"* And now Camila is the one shouting out for me to keep it down and stop screaming. Screaming? I think I might be the best shower singer out there despite what my family may say—just don't put me on a real stage in front of a real mic and audience!

Okay, fine, I'm no Marc Anthony, I get it, but music still has a prominent spot in my professional life. In addition to my having done several collaborations with Spotify, there is not a month that goes by without me featuring music in some way in one of my videos, be it singing in the shower, dancing on the kitchen counter with my mom to celebrate the Dominican Republic's independence, or collaborating with amazing artists like Jerry Rivera and La India, which have been opportunities I never would've dreamed of when I was blaring their songs as a kid. I mean, come on, Jerry's a Puerto Rican icon who I constantly listened to as a teen blinded by love: *"un amor como el nuestro, no debe morir jamás."* And who better to voice anger and frustration about love than La India and her powerhouse voice? If a Hispanic woman has La India on full blast, don't walk, run away as quick and far from her as you can. Hurry, because La India kills men with her songs—*"insoportable como amigo, insufrible como amor"*—absolutely priceless. These artists' songs have a prominent place in my heart; they've helped give voice to my emotions when nothing else seemed to do the trick.

But, wait, I don't just listen to salsa, bachata, and merengue, though I do love those genres deeply. Like most Hispanics, I enjoy a variety of music. I'll pump up the volume to Earth, Wind & Fire's "September" song in September and sing it like I'm one of the members of the band, and I will dance, jump around, and run in place to "I Need a Hero" while playing the Just Dance videogame and totally drop the mic at the end. Music makes me want to dance, smile, and sing. There's a song for every occasion and every mood, so much so that many of us choose what we listen to solely based on how we're feeling.

## Music Is Our Mood Identifier

Music is so interwoven in our lives that we don't only use it to do house chores and shower and party, we also use it to define, enhance, and ultimately express our mood, our current emotional state of being. When we find a lyric that captures what we are feeling in that instant, it's like hitting the jackpot. We know that song will be on repeat until we've finished celebrating our achievements or are done working through the sadness, anger, or frustration that has been eating us up inside. Singing those lyrics out loud to ourselves, to our families, to our lovers is better than going to therapy—it *is* our therapy. Music helps us rejoice, share our emotions, or simply comfort and heal a broken heart.

I met my first official girlfriend in high school. She was the first girl I brought home to meet my parents, and the first girl I fell in love with, and I thought that was it, she was the one. I was head over heels and blinded by profound emotions I had never experienced before. It was so powerful that when she broke up with me six months into our relationship, it was like the end of the world. My first love suddenly became my first big heartbreak, and it was torturous.

Love is the strongest emotion you can feel until you no longer have it. I was hit with a new and unfamiliar wave of emotions, ranging from complete heartbreak to utter despair. I had never been so devastated and depressed, silently weeping in my bed wondering if I would ever feel normal again. My family was steadfast by my side, handing me Kleenex, comforting me, pampering me with my favorite foods, telling me to snap out of it, and giving me hugs when I most needed them. I will never forget their kindness and unconditional love and support. They helped me pick up the broken pieces of my heart, and music helped me heal it. I didn't recognize myself, I didn't know how to act, I didn't know how to verbalize my pain, but music led the way. Songs are cathartic. They may seem like a form of torture for others, but if we've bottled up our emotions, we know that certain songs will help us cry it out and move on, and those lyrics let us know that we are not alone. When we realize that even our favorite singers have had to battle through heartbreak and have survived, there's a priceless glimmer of hope for our own days ahead. If they can do it, so can we. After I'd let it all out with a playlist filled with tearjerkers, then came the next one filled with hope, with the idea of a new love, with the promise of a better tomorrow, and once again, all was right in the world.

It's not just about the melody, it's about those wonderful lyrics that put your feelings into words. The lyrics of tunes that take you back to that first kiss or heartbreak, the first time you went to a baseball game with your dad, or the first time you drove a car by yourself. Songs are mega reminiscence makers. That's why it kills me when someone doesn't know the lyrics to my favorite jams. Okay, I'm not going to pretend I always know the lyrics to the songs I sing in my car or at home, because I don't. I've botched my fair share of tunes. But if I do know all the words, having someone babbling along at full volume to one of my songs drives me crazy. It used to happen with my sister all the time. I'd cut her off and say, "Look, you really need to stop until you know the song." Don't ruin it for me! The thing is, when you've taken the time to listen to the song on repeat and put in the attention until the lyrics are drilled into your head, a song takes on a new level of importance. Now you not only know the song, but are prepared to show off your skills; you are ready to perform it in front of the world (or at least in front of your family). "Hold up, turn it up, I'm about to kill this." And off you go!

We don't need a reason to put on music; we don't need a party or a special occasion. It is bigger than that, it is part of who we are, and that's why when we hang out with friends who don't listen to music, it gets super weird, super quick. That awkward moment of unnerving silence during a lull in a conversation, we just can't take it. *¡Música, maestro, por favor! Salsa, merengue, lo que sea, ¡wepa!* Music is our life.

# #FoodIsLove

*¡YA ESTÁ LA COMIDA!* When you hear that sentence yelled out in a Hispanic home, you are expected to drop what you're doing, sprint to the dining room table, and take your seat. Yes, even if you're on the phone with someone important, in the middle of writing down a genius idea that could make you a millionaire, or watching the last five minutes of the series finale of your favorite show—all of those things will have to wait, because the food cannot get cold. However, when you reach the table, don't be surprised if it is devoid of a meal. Your mom (or abuela) knows who she's dealing with, so she starts calling out to everyone a few minutes before she is actually ready. She is good like that, giving you plenty of time to heed her call. That's why if you are not there, ready and waiting, by the time she brings the food to the table, she will storm over to your room and deliver an earful of threats until you move your

behind to your designated seat. *"Te necesito aquí ahora."* No ifs or buts, just do it.

You have been called to the table, the sacred place in the Hispanic house, where families gather to pray, thank God for our food, eat, and gush about the meal before us, which has been prepared with so much love. It's where we laugh, argue, problem-solve, share ideas, recall anecdotes—it is our quintessential family time.

When I was growing up, our dinners together were always a big deal. First off, Hispanics dedicate so much time and effort in the kitchen that they turn every night into a feast of rice, beans, an assortment of meats, and salads. It's a colorful exploration of our heritage, a rainbow of *sazón* that dances on our palates and brings joy and tranquility to our souls. Regardless of what may have gone down in each of our days, we always came together at night for that precious quality time during dinner. And it didn't just involve eating and reiterating what we did earlier. The conversation flowed freely, unstructured, wherever our hearts desired. It wasn't scripted; it was about sharing what was on our minds on that particular evening. It could have been about our day, something in the news, something from the past, or about our families on the islands. One subject naturally led to another, transforming each night into a unique, unexpected, and oftentimes memorable moment.

Nevertheless, there is one holy rule we must all respect if we hope to taste our moms' next meal: we must always compliment the chef. One of the first questions that comes out of my mom's mouth after we put the first bite of food into our mouths is an eager *"¿Te gustó la comida? ¿Quedó buena?"* She is fishing for compliments, and we are there to deliver. *"Te quedó deliciosa"* is a good and solid answer. And be warned, do not fall for the *"Sí, pero creo que me quedaron un poquito saladitas las habichuelas."* Do not, under any circumstances, agree with her. Do not say, "Yeah, they could've used less salt." Never! She will always downplay her cooking just a little bit as a cue for you to add an enthusiastic *"¡Nooo, están riquísimas!"* Keep the comments positive, even if you are not crazy about that particular meal, because the food on our tables is not there just to nurture us physically, it is also a form of love. And when you shower your mom or your abuela with compliments about what she cooked that night, you are giving that love right back to her.

We are actually so used to praising the food we are served that it has become second nature. The plate of food set before us will receive some type of positive comment regardless of whether we are at home, at a family member's house, or at a restaurant. And when eating out, if we really like the dish we ordered, we must share it with everyone else. "Here, you need to try this," and before you can say, "Nah, I'm good," there's a forkful of someone else's entrée on your plate ready for your tasting. Then, with our mouths full and our food halfway finished, it is very likely we will launch into what we are craving for our next meal. That's how much we love our food, and that's why picky eaters have a difficult time at our tables.

Avoid Hispanic dinner invites if you have major food restrictions or are on a diet, because you will be offered what you cannot eat regardless of how thoroughly you have explained your reasons for this aforementioned "choice." If a Hispanic mom or abuela has cooked a meal and you reject it, it's like spitting in her face and outright rejecting her love. You just don't do that. It really is a lose-lose situation. If you politely serve yourself a small portion, she will immediately assume you don't like the food and comment on it out loud in front of you and everyone else at the table. *"Hmmm, a Carmencita como que no le gustó la comida."* No explanations will suffice by this point; it is too late. If you swing by your abuela's house and mention you are on a diet when she offers you a bite to eat, she will still pull out the flan or homemade *pastelillos* and offer them to you. *"Mi niño, cómete un chin, que te quiero ver fuerte."* She is your diet's worst enemy, the ultimate temptress. If you happen to face the same circumstances at your mom's house, when you cave and savor a bite of her delicacy, she may turn around and say, *"Pero es verdad que te hace falta perder un poquito de peso,"* commenting on how you could lose a few pounds. Because as much as your mom likes to feed you, she also has no qualms about giving it to you straight when it comes to your weight. Like I said, it's a lose-lose situation. So just bite the bullet, or that delicious *quesito*, and enjoy the moment. You can work it off tomorrow!

Some of our dinners may be short and sweet, while others may evolve into long after-dinner conversations while we are still sitting at the dining room table. However long our sit-downs may be, these are treasured bonding moments. This also means that excusing ourselves is unacceptable. Leaving early is just a big no-no in Hispanic etiquette at the dinner table. I know this may sound strange to non-Hispanics, but we are taught

### Picnic Time!

Food is so important to us, it goes beyond the dinner table and into everywhere we go. If we're off to the park, we're packing a picnic; if we're hopping on a plane, we're packing a picnic; if we're off to the beach, we're packing a picnic; if we're off on a four-hour road trip, we're packing a picnic; if we're going downstairs to the pool, we're packing a picnic. We can't go anywhere without a bite to eat at hand; it brings us comfort, joy, and security. Regardless of what may go wrong, we will not go hungry. Furthermore, since we know there is really nothing like our homemade food, it is quite common to spend the previous day cooking up a storm to make sure there's enough for everyone during the following day's outing. Yes, it's that important to us.

that it is plain disrespectful. Dinner is meant to be shared with family up until the last morsel on every plate has disappeared. So what do we do? We wait. We wait for everyone to finish their plates of food, we wait for dessert, and we wait for the *cafecito*. We wait until our parents give us the signal that it is okay to get up, which is when they start clearing the table. It may sound tedious to be glued to your seat for who knows how long, but the conversations and laughter that can unfold make that sacred family time incredibly worthwhile.

When I recall my family dinners while I was growing up, I can easily picture all of us sitting at our round table, sharing different moods and thoughts, talking, and joking. I can see the countless meals at different stages of my life, as a kid being told to finish my plate of food, as a reluctant and rebellious preteen hoping my mom and I didn't get into another argument, and as a young adult having cool conversations, being silly, listening attentively, and cherishing every second of our time together. Meals are unique and beautiful rituals that are all about love. The love that goes into making each of our favorite dishes, the love and satisfaction of having enough to feed the whole family, the love that is shared while sitting together at every meal. The significance of our food goes beyond our need to take in calories to survive. Food is strength, food is prosperity, food is health, and ultimately, food is love.

# #ElBochinche

A S LOVING AND caring and supportive as our families are, they also looove to *bochinchar*. *"¿Tú sabías que la hija de María todavía no se ha casado? Si no se apura se va a quedar jamona."* As if María's relationship status is anyone's business. However, nothing can be done. There will always be that one aunt, or cousin, or uncle, or even grandparent who will be stirring the pot with behind-the-scenes comments dropped in the kitchen or on the phone. Some people may refer to this as *el qué dirán*, but to me it boils down to *el bochinche*, or good old-fashioned behind-the-back gossip.

*El bochinche* is so prevalent it infiltrates every aspect of our life, yet no one ever wants to be the center of that gossip. To avoid this predicament, there are necessary precautions that every family takes, which usually come in the form of exhaustive criticism. If you post a picture online that your parents don't approve of, they will call you immediately to ask you to take it down: *"Niño, borra esa foto, que pareces un loco."* They obviously know you're not crazy, but other people who see you looking like that might start saying otherwise, and that is unacceptable. So our parents are always paying extra attention to what we do on the Internet to help safeguard us from unnecessary evils, but the secret truth is that they're also watching out for themselves. Because whatever we do, say, or post ultimately comes back to haunt them as a reflection of their parental skills.

Enter our need to always look sharp. It's not just that we Hispanics value cleanliness to an obsessive degree, it is also because doing so helps ward off the busybodies. I learned this the hard way in Puerto Rico. My school uniform required me to wear white polo shirts, which was fine until the recess bell rang and I ran out to play with all the other kids. Clearly, by the end of the day, when I walked through our front door, my shirt was stained, and I got scolded as if I'd done it on purpose. "You need to make sure you look clean at all times" was my mom's final pronouncement. Really? I was only six years old. How did she expect me to stay clean and have fun at recess with my friends? *"Fácil.* Wear an undershirt beneath your white polo, then take off the polo and put it in your backpack before heading out to play with the other kids." The sweltering heat was not her problem, what people said if I walked down the street with a dirty shirt was. End of story.

When summer rolled around and I was dropped off at the San Juan airport to catch a flight to Santo Domingo with my grandparents, I always got the same speech from my mom. "Don't forget to shower, make sure you are always clean, wear your best clothes, and look sharp, because the last thing I want to hear is that I have a slob for a kid." Of course, I was also told to behave, respect my elders, and so on and so forth. "*Sí*, Mami, don't worry." But worry she did, because she knew that if I wasn't extra careful, I could easily take center stage in one of my tía's spins around the gossip wheel.

Naturally, after we've practiced such precise methods of upkeep, looking clean and sharp becomes second nature in the Hispanic community; it is something we take pride in; and it is something that we will continue to hear about from our families if we at any point let go or slip up. That's what inspired the video with the daughter heading out the door to run an errand not caring that her hair is completely disheveled. *"Niña, ¿cómo vas a salir a la calle así? ¡Pareces una loca!"* The mom goes off on her because she knows that if someone from their circle recognizes her daughter on the street and sees her looking like that, it will come back to haunt her. *"¿Cómo la dejas salir así?"* she demands, as if her grown daughter's appearance, or lack thereof, is her fault.

Keeping up appearances is so important that even my abuela Carlita, minutes before being rolled into the operating room for one of her brain cancer surgeries, turned to us and asked that we make sure to keep her hair short and well trimmed. The last thing she wanted was to look crazy for the nurses taking care of her at the hospital. God forbid they see her hair out of place! Obviously, we did exactly as we were told, because we understood that this was a legitimate concern. Looking good is something we enjoy, it makes us feel put together and proud. So much so that our elder family members always make sure they're looking fly before leaving the house. Cute outfit, hair done, makeup on, and out the door. It's not that we're frivolous. It's about looking decent and presentable, and doing everything in our power to elude our family's critical eye.

## Tough Love

There are no filters in the Hispanic family. Call it criticism, tough love, or what you may, if you are out of sorts in any way, your family will let you know—big-time. They will be the first ones to offer you food and give you an attitude if you don't eat while also letting you know that you should watch your figure if you want to get a man or woman. They will tell you that your new haircut isn't doing you any favors, and if you counter with "Well, at least my girlfriend likes it," they'll reply, *"Sí, pero con ese pelo no creo que te dure mucho."* It's really a no-win situation. No matter what you say or do, the minute you walk into a room full of family, someone is going to shout out something about the way you look that will sting. The truth is nothing hurts more than your family criticizing you, but it still happens constantly in our gatherings. And you know when it's coming too. You can detect it in their faces, and all that is left for you to do is take a breath and think, *Okay, here we go, let me have it and let's get this over with.*

"*Uy, chica, ese* lipstick *como que te queda feo.*" There's no turning around and changing your makeup now.

*"¿Y esa ropa? ¿Tú vas pa' la casa de tu abuela así?"* In this case, if you still have a chance to rush back to your closet and change into something your family might approve of, do it!

*"Ve arreglándote ese pelo, que no me gusta."* Crazy hairstyles are usually frowned upon in our generally more conservative-leaning families.

*"Tú como que estás más gordito. ¡Tienes que dejar de comer!"* But you better eat what's being served that day even if your family does think you've put on some weight.

Gotta give this one to Americans. They are more reserved, and we may criticize this sometimes, but, man, do I appreciate it within this context. Close American friends or relatives may pull you aside and suggest you hit the gym with them to get in better shape, but they'd never walk up to you in a roomful of people and yell out, "Duuude, you are looking fat today! And you, girrrrl, you better lay off the food if you want to find a boyfriend!" Reading it in English makes you cringe, doesn't it? But in Spanish, it is so normal that we don't even think twice about it. *"¡Wow, tú sí que estás comiendo bien!"* or *"Ese vestido te queda apretaito."* Well, there's no changing the dress now, so you have to live with it for the rest of the night, uncomfortably tugging at the tight spots in the hope that no one else will drop a comment like that again. Talk about a mood killer! However, let it be said, we will always prefer this type of in-your-face criticism to the one that goes down behind our backs.

Now you know why Hispanic women struggle so much with what to wear before heading to a family gathering. They need to find the perfect outfit that strikes the balance between trendy and respectable, so that if they happen to fall under the spotlight it is because they look fabulous. Because we all know that the minute we walk into that room, as we say hello to each person individually, we are being scrutinized from head to toe—hair, face, weight, makeup, clothes, shoes, and God forbid you have a new piercing or tattoo popping out from under your sleeve. When my parents discovered my tattoos, they basically hated me for months. It was as if I had done it on purpose to hurt them. I tried to show them that I actually had the tats done to honor my family: two roses, one with my mom's name and the other with Abuela Carlita's. But that was meaningless in their eyes. A tattoo is a tattoo, and mine were a disgrace to the family. Of course, what followed was the assumption that I had started hanging out with the wrong crowd—that ever-present "wrong crowd" that actually never existed within my circle of friends. But that didn't stop my parents from putting me under the microscope and—here we go again—lecturing me about the dangers of traveling that long and misguided road.

At the end of the day, as much as those critiques hurt, that is not their intention. Our Hispanic families are simply born without that filter. Yet, like everything we do, this criticism serves a purpose (remember, lessons are everywhere!). Our family members' outspoken observations toughen us up for the real world. When we walk outside, we unknowingly already carry the tools to help us deal with unexpected negative feedback or constructive criticism, or outright gossip. It's nothing new to us because we've been facing it since we were kids. And our families' criticism not only toughens us up, it keeps us humble. If you happen to walk into your house thinking you are all that and a bag of chips, someone in your family will take note and bring you back down to reality in a minute. They will always keep it real for us, and that is something we should cherish no matter how irked we are at our families' seemingly constant jabs.

Telling it like it is, whether we want to hear it or not, that's what our families do and that's why I ultimately see their comments as tough love. If we follow their advice, keep our hair neat, stop wearing ridiculous outfits, and lose a little weight, it will not only benefit us in the long run, but also will steer us clear from being the center of a family member's *bochinche* and save our parents from disgrace in the process. There we go, now that's a win-win situation, however twisted it may sound. At the end of the day, our families have no qualms about criticizing us, but having others do the same is unacceptable. If all else fails, our parents know there's still one more option to deter *las malas lenguas*: shift the attention to our accomplishments and bring on the bragging.

## Bragging Rights

Our people talk a lot. So if we want to help our parents redirect *el bochinche*, we have to give them something to brag about. Having good brag-worthy achievements under your belt will not only save you from some of the irritating tough love, but also give your parents tools to put an uplifting spin on all the chitchat and relieve you from the mood-killing critiques. So if you go from being single to having a girlfriend, boom, they've got something to brag about with the rest of the family. If you've recently landed a job, great, another brag-worthy achievement. Started college recently? Fantastic, let the bragging begin.

Parents and grandparents in particular cherish their bragging rights so much that sometimes it feels like they may have had you and your siblings only so they could eventually have someone to brag about. And brag they will, to their family, friends, the bank teller, the post office worker, and anyone who is willing to listen. They like showing off the family résumé with a long list of achievements. Last time we went to Puerto Rico, my mom couldn't stop gushing about me to all of her friends and family. And I was right there, standing in front of them! But that made no difference. It was so embarrassing, but I also know that bragging is a right our parents have earned, and all we can do is grin and bear it, and be grateful that they are bragging rather than criticizing us.

When all is said and done, Hispanic parents are incredibly proud of their children. The best way we can thank them for their sacrifices is by showing them, with the lives we lead, that their hard work and tough love paid off. None of us want our parents to feel ashamed of us, none of us want them to be in the *bochinche* spotlight; we want to do right by our moms and dads and make them as proud as can be. Because when they are proud, when they express their joy about our accomplishments, that is the ultimate high—and, personally, that's what really makes me happy.

# #HispanicFamilyGatherings

HISPANICS DON'T NEED a special occasion to get together; any excuse will do. We are super social people who love hanging out in family settings and generally love company, so we're around each other all the time. If a few people drop in for a visit, an average day can turn into a party in a microsecond. Suddenly, someone is placing food on the table, someone else is firing up the grill, music starts playing, laughter is ringing in the air, and eventually a couple of people will bounce up from their chairs to dance a few bars of their favorite tune. I love that this is a cultural trait we share across the board in Latin America and as Hispanics here in the United States; it's a true privilege to be a part of such a close-knit community. And guess what? You can be a part of it too if you're not Hispanic, because one basic rule we all have in common is that our doors are always open to everyone.

Call it the immigrant experience or the Hispanic generosity of spirit, or maybe it's a combination of both, but if you have no place to go, you are always welcome in our homes. Our gatherings are not just for family, but also for friends. We will make sure to feed you and make you feel at home. Be prepared to receive a lot of love. We are very affectionate people, which you can see even in the way we greet each other. When we meet up, there is always a kiss on the cheek or a hug hello before we start any conversation, so don't be alarmed by this when you walk into our homes.

We tend to express our emotions on a physical level, not just by greeting you with a hug and kiss, but also by patting you on the back to see if you're okay, grabbing you by the arm and leading you into the kitchen to show you what we're proudly cooking, and/or taking you by the hand to our improvised dance floor in the living room and showing you how to salsa and merengue your way into our hearts. If we notice you making even an ounce of an effort to communicate with us, you will be cheered on and showered with good vibes. So, if you are not Hispanic, don't freak out about our need or desire to give affection. We are not coming on to you, we are just literally welcoming you with open arms. It's one of the ways we communicate. Although sometimes, out of context, it can put us in awkward situations.

When greeting Americans, we honestly never quite know if we should go in for a kiss on the cheek, a hug, a pat on the back, a firm handshake, or just a quick wave of the hand and a mouthed "hi" from a respectable distance. Our instinct is to go all in as usual, but that can get awkward real quick. I try to assess the situation and am usually good at picking out the people who aren't used to our type of affectionate greeting, but sometimes I miss the mark. I did it the other day, while meeting the fiancée of one of my favorite basketball players for the first time. I was overcome by the excitement of the game that had just ended, and my natural instinct kicked in, so I leaned in for a quick kiss on the cheek while saying, "Hey, nice to meet you." That's when I realized I had unintentionally breached her personal space. She tensed up and gave me that look I've seen so many times before when growing up Hispanic in the United States, that look that says, "What the hell do you think you're doing?" Fortunately, she didn't say anything, she just stood there, and I didn't know where to hide. I don't think it even lasted a minute, but it felt like an eternity.

I should've known better, but I got caught up in the moment and completely forgot American protocol. When we wobble into a room as toddlers, the first thing we're taught is to kiss every-one hello. It's plain old manners in our book. We are incredibly affectionate people and we wear our emotions on our sleeves. Maybe that's why others see us as hotheaded, hot-blooded, passionate Latinos. And they're right. We are not afraid of our emotions. Our tears rush down our cheeks freely when we are upset or emotional, whether we are men or women. Our loud laughter fills the room when we are having a good time. And when we love, we love hard. I'm not talking just about relationships. I'm talking about relatives and friends, and friends who become relatives. Because after a while, our close friends slowly morph into family. That's why you'll see us refer to a bunch of people as our tías, tíos, and primos, even though they are not our aunts, uncles, or cousins by blood. They are just friends who were brought into the fold a while back and have been family ever since. Once you're in the circle, all your future generations are part of the family too: kids, grandkids, and so forth.

So, yes, although we tend to have big families, if you dig a little deeper at one of our gatherings, you will always find a few people who are relatives by friendship rather than blood. Consider yourself warned. When you walk into a Hispanic home, there's always a chance you will walk out with a new family. That's what unites us and makes us so strong as a community, regardless of what country we may come from.

## Sporting Events: Pick a Team

As open and loving as we are, when it comes to sports, all bets are off. I don't care if you are my friend, cousin, sister, or father, if we are not rooting for the same team, then we are mortal enemies for the duration of the game or season. The passion for sports fuels us, and it is another great reason for get-togethers with friends and family. What's the fun in rooting for a team in an empty room without being able to shout out to our uncles that their team could use a new coach, or to sit beside our dads and pick apart the game like professional sports analysts? Yes, we take our sports incredibly seriously. It is a way of life. Baseball, basketball, football, soccer—you name it, I love it.

Sports are such a big part of our lives that kids, especially boys, find the most common question they are asked at a family gathering is "So what do you play?" That's right, no one bothers to ask you *if* you play a sport, it is automatically assumed that you do, so they just want to know which one to get into that topic with you, find out how your team is doing, when you're playing, and if you're thinking of going pro. My sport was baseball. Even though I wasn't that great at it, I loved it and became a huge sports fan in general because of it and my family. It's hard not to in Hispanic families. We grow up seeing our parents passionately cheer on their teams: *"¡Vamos arriba, hay que ganar este juego!"* We learn the superstitions to follow—like sitting in the same seat, wearing a specific jersey, saying a prayer, or in my brother's case, holding a rosary each time LeBron is competing in the playoffs. We're dressed up in the team colors, so it's impossible not to absorb at the very least a little bit of this love of sports. And this love is passed down from generation to generation, together with the family team. If your parents have always loved the Yankees, then you were likely dressed up in Yankee gear as a baby and have a jersey or hat stashed away somewhere because your duty is to love them just as hard. If they are Red Sox fans, you will proudly be donning your Sox hat, even when you visit family in New York, and you should know all about the Curse of the Bambino and the day the Sox finally broke it.

We love our sports so much that some Latin American countries come to a complete standstill when their national teams are playing, especially when it's *fútbol* and they're playing in the World Cup. Everyone is at home with family glued to the TV.

Businesses close and it is treated almost like a national holiday. The streets are so quiet you could hear a pin drop. And when its team scores a goal, the entire country explodes in celebration.

During these specific types of family gatherings, we all love to chime in with our two cents, as if we know better than the commentators, players, or coaches themselves. Part of watching sports together is breaking down the game and analyzing every move. Suddenly we are all experts. And when a play doesn't work or a goal isn't scored, we become merciless, immediately firing coaches and players left and right in our minds to create the winning team of our dreams. I can't even begin to imagine how hard it must be to be a Latin American athlete—they are constantly being scrutinized by their fans. However, similar to the criticism that surfaces at our family gatherings, the fans' nitpickiness is closely tied to their die-hard love for their team.

When we support a team, we do so wholeheartedly, and that's another reason watching games together is so exciting for us. The game's outcome will dictate the rest of our day and week. We prep for the day, dress in our team jerseys, follow the necessary superstitions, and cook up a feast for our guests. As the game unfolds, we talk, laugh, hold our breath, cheer, get angry, become quiet and sullen, burst into celebration, all depending on how our team is playing. By the end of the day, if our team wins, we feel so rewarded that we want to keep the party going all night long. However, God forbid our team loses. The spirited family gathering suddenly becomes a solemn funeral. If my team loses a big championship, rest assured I will enter into mourning and it will affect the remainder of my week; that's how passionate I am about sports. This passion may affect not only our days but also our relationships with friends or relatives supporting the opposing team. Sports create the ultimate Hispanic rivalry, and all bets are off. I just love it. Watching a game is a fantastic time to share with friends and family. We are extremely passionate people, that's for sure, and that passion comes through in our sports gatherings just as much as it does during the holidays—another moment where we go all out.

## The Holidays: Go Big or Go Home

We celebrate more holidays than anyone I know. Really, there always seems to be a reason to have a day off. In Puerto Rico and the Dominican Republic alone, there are so many holidays that I can't even keep track of them. Each one is the perfect reason for families to gather—we are party people, after all—but none are as significant, critical, and all-important as the end-of-year trifecta: Thanksgiving, Christmas, and New Year's Eve.

First off, the prep begins weeks in advance of each celebration. We stress out, get organized, and figure out the guest list and who's bringing what type of food or drink. With such a large crowd, everyone is expected to pitch in. As you can imagine, or as you well know, food is everywhere on these special dates: small snacks in the living room, side dishes set up in the dining room, the main feast being finalized in the kitchen. Wherever you turn, someone nearby has a small plate in hand and is nibbling on something delicious and sipping on some *coquito* while waiting for the main course to be served. Meanwhile, there's always some tío telling inappropriate jokes in one corner, a few cousins and a tía gossiping on the couch and looking over their shoulders to make sure the person in question can't hear them, another tío and some dads trying to work the stereo, an abuelo dozing off in a chair, and our moms and abuelas fervently making the remaining dishes while chitchatting with the passersby and offering them small tastes of the feast to come.

These celebrations are brimming with music, intermittent dancing, and endless reminiscing. They are times to catch up with relatives, talk politics and current events, share memories and make new ones, offer up nuggets of wisdom, and hear outrageous stories about your parents, aunts, and uncles from when they were young and reckless, something that to the younger generations is hard to fathom. And if you think you are going to be spared, you better think twice, because when you least expect it, an embarrassing story from your childhood will surface, one that will make you turn bright red and pray it is over soon. *"Te recuerdas cuando Juan pensó que podía . . ."* No one is safe from these public revelations; it's part of our tradition!

The holiday atmosphere really takes over our lives. Each celebration has a certain vibe, specific decorations, and menus to fit the tradition of the occasion. The end-of-year trifecta are extra-special holidays, so our outfits aim to impress . . . because you know we all want to look *guapo* for the classic family portraits and all the pics taken by everyone's candid camera. And although we stick to traditions, we also Hispanify each event to give it our own special twist.

Take Thanksgiving, for example. At home, Mami always makes

the classic turkey, but roasting right next to it in the oven is our beloved *pernil* (pork), because no holiday is right without a *pernil asado*. We usually do away with the yams, mashed potatoes, and cranberry sauce, and replace them with rice and ham, *arroz con gandules*, sliced avocado, empanadas, *plátanos fritos*, *ensalada verde*, and *ensalada rusa*. And instead of the pies, we have flan and an assortment of other Puerto Rican and Dominican desserts. Thanksgiving is also the unofficial kickoff to the Christmas season at home, which means this is the weekend we set up and decorate our Christmas tree, to be enjoyed throughout December and sometimes well into January too.

This takes me back to when we were living in Puerto Rico. As soon as December rolled in, the *parranderos*—the Caribbean version of Christmas carolers—would hit the streets. They would gather together to surprise friends by setting up outside their homes with instruments, yelling out *"¡Asalto!"* and singing. If you're serenaded by *parranderos*, as soon as you hear them, tradition calls for you to open the door and invite them in. They'll continue to sing and play inside while you bring out snacks and drinks to feed them. So December is also a time when your fridge has to be constantly brimming with food because you never know when a *parranda* will come calling at your door.

I can't even begin to imagine the trouble *parranderos* would get into here in the United States. Because I'm not talking about a group of mellow Christmas carolers, I'm talking about a raucous band playing instruments and singing at full force, basically performing a live concert outside your front door. The public disturbance complaints from our neighbors would be off the charts!

Then comes Christmas. The feast is similar to our Thanksgiving meal, but all eyes and efforts are on Christmas Eve, the main event for Hispanics, the evening we most look forward to during the holiday season. We wake up that day with eager anticipation, prepping whatever's needed to make the night a special one. Relatives fly in from other parts of the country or the islands just to be together during this monumental celebration. When day turns into night, we all emerge from our rooms dressed in elegant attire with some sort of red or green to reflect the specific holiday, our hair coiffed, ready to pray, eat, drink, and be merry with our loved ones. Meanwhile, the main goal—especially for children—is to reach midnight. Why? Because that's when we open our gifts! We don't wait till Christmas morning, like most Americans. The stroke of midnight is our definitive cue to rejoice—"*¡Feliz Navidad!*"—and head straight over to the carefully selected presents.

I love this tradition, but maybe that's because it's what I'm used to. However, just the thought of being a kid having to go to sleep and wait till the next morning to get my presents seems like pure torture. How do you know when it's okay to open the presents? Do you have to wait for everyone else to get up? Does an adult give you the green light? No way, not for me. The sooner the better, and knowing the exact time removes some of the impending anxiety. All that's left, especially for the kids and the elders, is to do our best to stay awake until twelve, which only adds to the challenge and excitement. Post–gift exchange, we chitchat some more and then call it a night, exhausted by the excitement and still stuffed from all the food. Christmas Day for us is chill. We'll hang out in our pajamas, eat leftovers from the night before, watch movies, check out our gifts more carefully, and gossip about the night before.

As if all this celebrating weren't enough, we have one more biggie to look forward to: New Year's Eve. Another huge gathering, another over-the-top celebration, another similar spread of food and drinks, and the night when we wear our sharpest outfits to ring in the New Year in style. Traditions for New Year's Eve vary among our different countries, but they don't just involve the final countdown to midnight. No, our countdown is accompanied by rituals that we follow to a tee. The gobbling down of the twelve grapes, one at each stroke of midnight, to bring us good luck in the New Year is a classic at my house. We've also done the dressing in white ritual, to absorb positive vibes for the New Year. But it doesn't stop there. I've heard of people putting on yellow underwear for good fortune, red if they want to find love, eating a spoonful of lentils for prosperity, and running around the block with a suitcase packed with items that represent the destinations they'd like to travel to. The list goes on and on. Can you imagine being in a house that follows all of these rituals? Quick, eat the grapes! Here's your lentils! Now go, go, go, and don't forget your suitcase!

Fortunately, the only thing my mom insists on every year is the grapes. But the best part for me, the one moment that I cherish the most, is when the clock strikes twelve and we all sing out, *"¡Feliz Año Nuevo!"* and proceed to hug each person in the room, exchanging meaningful good wishes for the New Year. My mom always holds me in her arms and says a prayer in my ear, wishing me health, happiness, and prosperity. She's followed by my dad, who hugs me tight and whispers his own wishes for my well-being. I respond in kind, following their lead, and am always moved beyond words. Those blessings stay with me for the rest of the year, and now I make it a point to choose my own message carefully for each relative, to give back the positive energy released by such wonderful sentiments at the start of the year. They set the stage for the months ahead. Exchanging New Year's blessings is so deep and beautiful, and something I wish more of us took upon ourselves to do and to pass on as a tradition.

How about the next time your American neighbors freak out about the twentysomething cars parked outside your driveway and threaten to call the police, you don't just tell them it's a family gathering but invite them in, so they too can experience the holidays the way we do. Show them that there's nothing to fear; we're all about family, love, laughter, communication, food, and the joy of being together. *Eso sí*, if they dare say yes to this invite, make sure to prep them for the experience with the following survival strategies.

## Top Five Hispanic Gathering Survival Strategies

Hispanics are a loud, filterless, emotional, and loving bunch of people. It is fantastic. I wouldn't have it any other way. It is who we are, all the way from the southern tip of Argentina to the northern tip of Mexico and on all of our Caribbean islands, but come on . . . you know we can also be outlandishly overwhelming. So to all my beloved non-Latinos, if you're ever invited to a Hispanic family gathering, use the following top five strategies as your survival guide so you can take it all in stride like a Hispanic pro! For the rest of us, use this as a good refresher course, a reminder of what's to come and how to deal with it.

## 1. DRESS TO IMPRESS, BUT DON'T GO OVERBOARD

As discussed in "#ElBochinche," appearance is never overlooked by our community. Finding a flattering and appropriate outfit for the occasion is key to receiving compliments and avoiding the criticism spotlight. If it's an everyday gathering, all you have to worry about is looking clean and put together. If it's a special occasion (birthday, big holiday, graduation), then definitely slide into something a bit more elegant and sharp, because the occasion will be immortalized in a thousand photos that will later be shared online, printed, framed, and set on someone's mantelpiece for the world to see.

## 2. TIMING YOUR ARRIVAL JUST RIGHT

Yes, arriving fashionably late is acceptable at our gatherings, but you have to be careful with your timing. Sure, you don't want to be the first one through the door, but if you are one of the last to arrive, you are in for a major greeting operation. Don't expect to get away with walking in and waving a generic hello to cover your bases—you will be met by deathly stares screaming, *"¿Y este quién se cree?"* and an uncomfortable silence because that does not fly in our homes. You are expected to say hello to each individual at our gatherings with a hug or a kiss, followed by your name to those you don't know. If you're Hispanic, you know the drill, but don't forget to say *"Bendición"* to your elders! *Bendición*, next, *bendición*, repeat.

### 3. EXTRA POINTS FOR PARTICIPATION

Remember, our gatherings are first and foremost times for sharing and catching up with loved ones you don't get to see on a regular basis, so everyone is expected to make an effort to chat with everyone else, even if only for a quick "Hey, how've you been?" exchange. If you're there with a friend and don't know anyone, don't be afraid to start up a random conversation. It will be much appreciated and incredibly well received. As for the kids of the family hosting the gathering, do not, by any means, hide in your room. Come on, you should know better. Aside from being *una falta de respeto*, avoiding the guests is just plain rude, and you may be attracting a future *pela* if you do so. So put on your best smile and get down to socializing. You'll be surprised, eventually you may even realize that you are actually . . . wait for it . . . having fun!

## 4. How to Deal with
## Unsolicited Advice

Okay, this one is a biggie. It's something we all dread about our beloved family gatherings. As wonderful, colorful, and joyful as these get-togethers may be, they are also rife with criticism, tough love, and unsolicited advice. Everyone will be up in your business within a minute of your arrival. Expect to be grilled to the core on certain topics and receive solutions you didn't even realize you needed for problems you thought were secret. That's your first mistake right there. We don't keep secrets. Everyone in the family knows what's going on in your life, and if they think they have a good piece of advice for you, they will not hesitate to approach you and make it known for all to hear, regardless of whether it falls within their realm of expertise or not. *"A fulanito le pasó lo mismo. ¿Sabes lo que hizo él?"* No need to answer, because they're going to tell you anyway. That's just the way it is. Your problem will be discussed in the family's public forum, take it or leave it. It's annoying and loving and hilarious, if you are able to take a step back and observe it from a distance. Not so funny when you're the subject at hand, especially if you're a woman and "still single."

*"¿Y el novio?"* I always find this puzzling because I know how overprotective parents are with their girls, yet they are also constantly pushing them to find a man so they don't turn into *jamonas* for the rest of their lives. It makes no sense! Though now that I think of it, maybe it's just the parents fearing their daughters will be alone in the world when they die. Yeah, that

sounds about right. Whatever the reason, you have now been warned. If you are a single woman, you will be grilled about this topic to figure out if there's something wrong with you or something the family can do to help.

My advice? Let them talk and then say something like, *"No, Tía, estoy tranquila,* you know, focused on school and work," and then beeline it out of there as soon as possible. You can also deflect with humor: "You know me, *¡jamona para toda la vida, ja, ja, ja!"* and step away from the group, or ask someone else a personal or revelatory question to shift everyone's attention to the next victim and hightail it into the bathroom. By the time you come out, they will have moved on to something juicier.


## 5. RELAX AND ENJOY THE RIDE

At the end of the day, any excuse, big or small, is a good one for us to get together and for you to join us. Gathering around a table, in the living room, in the kitchen, out in the backyard, to eat, talk, and spend some quality time with our loved ones and new friends brings us enormous amounts of joy and solace. No matter how far from or close to our home countries we may be, we are all in this together, and nowhere can you feel this unifying fortress more than at a Hispanic gathering.

# #MamáHayUnaSola

I TAKE AFTER MY MOTHER. There's no denying it. I have her features, her temperament, and her comedic whim. When I think of my mom, I see a force to be reckoned with, a heart of gold, and the ultimate Superwoman. When I was growing up, she was the brain and powerhouse of our home, orchestrating our lives to ensure that every moving piece was functioning smoothly and that every one of us had all we needed to thrive. She would wake up at six in the morning, make breakfast, send us off to school with a kiss, and then head to work with my dad. Once they were done with their shifts, they'd pick us up at my grandparents' house and take us home. And as soon as she stepped through our front door, instead of putting her feet up and relaxing after a long day's work, my mom kept going. Regardless of what time it was, she would cook, tidy up the house, check in with her children to make sure we were all keeping up with our schoolwork and to gauge how we were doing on a personal level, while also spending quality time with my dad to continue nourishing their love and relationship, never missing a beat in the process.

As a child, I didn't realize how much Mami did for us and how much time and effort she dedicated to our well-being, but now I see it as clear as day. In Hispanic households, *la mamá es la que manda*, and my mom was no different. She was the head of the house, overseeing every aspect of our day-to-day lives, in sync with my dad, who followed her lead and supported her vision, yet acted more like the peacekeeper trying to find a happy medium for all of us to flourish. Their partnership is strong and healthy. In their thirty-nine years together, one has never been above the other; they are a team facing everything that comes their way as a united front, but my mom is usually the one calling the shots.

It's just a fact of life in Hispanic households. Although some assume our culture is rife with machismo, the truth hiding behind this stereotype is that we cannot function without the women in our lives—they are essential parts of our existence. Our moms are our rocks, our superheroes. If there's a crisis, they are never rattled; at least, not in front of us. Somehow they manage to pull it together, keep calm, transmit a sense of security and comfort, and take action, never letting on if they are actually panic-stricken and terrified on the inside. If we are hungry, they will not hesitate to give us the food off their plates. When we feel under the weather or need advice, the first people we turn to are our mothers. They are the ones standing on the sidelines ready to help us get up when we fall down; the ones who know us better than we know ourselves and have our best interests at heart; and they are there, every step of the way, as figures of unconditional love and support, sharing priceless nuggets of wisdom and teaching us invaluable lessons to be applied throughout our lives.

One of the first such lessons I learned from my mom is something that is a family tradition in many Latin American countries, especially Puerto Rico and the Dominican Republic: *pedir la bendición.* This is the way we are taught to greet our parents and grandparents and elderly loved ones; we are literally asking for their blessing, *"Bendición."* It's a sign of respect and humility to which they respond with *"Que Dios te bendiga,"* may God bless you. When I walk through the door at home or call my parents on the phone, *bendición* is the first word that comes out of my mouth.

It's a no-brainer now, but that's because I faced hell and high water as a kid when I happened to forget to utter this word and greet my mom with a kiss after coming home from school. *"Que muchacho más malcriado. ¿Cómo tú llegas de la escuela sin saludarme y perdir la bendición? ¡Que falta de respeto!"* What got into me and gave me the courage to dare walk into our home and not ask for her blessing and greet her like a normal human being? I was likely just having a bad day, but that was no excuse. If I made the mistake of not greeting my mom properly, her exclamation usually turned into a five-minute diatribe on my rudeness and absolute lack of respect and appreciation for everything she did for me, until I managed to reluctantly turn around, walk back to her side, and correct my actions with a hug and a kiss.

Saying *"Bendición"* and greeting my mom with an affectionate gesture was so drilled into my psyche that I felt incredibly uncomfortable when I followed my American friends into their houses and they completely ignored their moms or just waved a faraway hi in passing. That would not fly in my home. Hispanic moms are not to be ignored, and if you happen to make this mistake, you will be called out on it immediately.

The typical scenario where I sometimes walked in and pulled an American hi from afar was when I was too absorbed in my own world and problems to even realize I was committing this act of treason. But my mom quickly made me snap back to reality, teaching me that life goes beyond the walls of my mind and that taking others into account is just as important as figuring out my own problems. This realization is what led me to feature this topic in a couple of videos in the past few years. Because forgetting to greet our parents with *"Bendición"* or a simple *"Hola, ¿cómo estás?"* and its consequences is likely something that everyone in our Hispanic community has experienced firsthand. Rudeness is unacceptable. We are taught to put an effort into communicating and respecting our loved ones. Nowadays, I couldn't fathom living in a world where I didn't ask my mom for a *bendición* when I see her or call her and tell her that I love her when I leave home or hang up the phone.

*Pedir la bendición* is not only a greeting of love and gratitude toward our parents; it also serves as a dialogue opener, leading to additional communication that is vital to our everyday lives.

When you greet your mom, she uses this quick exchange to pick up on your vibe and see how you're doing. If all is well, she will let you go about your business, but if by chance you seem off to her in any way, this greeting gives her the perfect opportunity to pursue the conversation and get to the bottom of what's making you cranky or moody. Her follow-up questions may seem annoying, but chances are this talk will leave you feeling better than when you first walked in.

Hispanic mothers can sense how we're feeling from a mile away, even before we understand it ourselves. Their powerful intuition never ceases to amaze me; it is through the roof. It only takes a two-minute conversation with my mom for her to know if I'm mad, sad, or frustrated; if I don't feel like talking; if I'm tired or about to get a cold; or if I got into a fight with my fiancée. She picks up on my body language, my expressions, my choice of words, and assesses the situation in the blink of an eye. Even when I try my hardest to act normal, it is useless. I can't hide my feelings from her because she will switch into detective mode and sniff them out. It's like a superpower she has to decipher what's going on, reading between the lines and making me talk about it, even when I don't want to.

*"¿Todo bien, hijo?"* she'll ask innocently, knowing full well that all is not okay.

"Yeah, Mami. I'm here, *tranquilo*," I reply, hoping to get her off my back.

*"Ajá, ¿y cómo está Camila? ¿Y el trabajo?"*

The first line of questioning always involves relationships and work, the basics of our everyday lives. If I'm successful with my act, and Mami doesn't find the answers she's looking for, she will continue to pursue her interrogation, and that's when it clicks in my mind and I can't help but wonder, *How does she know?* Sometimes I don't even realize I'm in a funk until I face her inquiries. She pushes my buttons, but also helps me face and deal with my issues head-on.

As annoying as these questions may be, they come from a place of love and concern. Our moms are genuinely worried about us and want to figure out how they can help us. This realization is what drove me to make the video "When Hispanic Parents Ask You if Everything Is Okay in Your Relationship," featuring the mom subtly asking her annoyed and defensive daughter if she's doing okay, when she clearly knows her daughter is down about her relationship. I saw this play out all the time at home with my poor sister.

I understand now what Mami was doing, but I also vividly remember how it felt to be asked these questions when I was young, upset, and unable to understand or handle my emotions. I would shut down, not wanting to go there, but that didn't stop my mom from continuing to probe and finesse her way into the conversation. Our moms will get to the bottom of our issues. If one road doesn't lead to the answer, they will take as many alternative paths as needed and push as many buttons as are at their disposal to get us to finally spill the beans. This acknowledgment of the feelings they are hunting for doesn't have to be in the form of an outright confession. If one of their questions gets a strong reaction, that's all the proof they need to know what area in our lives is causing us discomfort. Because they know

## When Hispanic Moms Embarrass You

As fantastic as our moms are, with their superhero powers to get us all through the ups and downs of life, they can also embarrass the hell out of us. They're always in our business, giving us unsolicited advice that sometimes makes us turn bright red. They mispronounce words or names, and no matter how many times we try to teach them the right way to say "YonYon" is actually "John Young Parkway," we will get *"Ay, tú me entiendes"* as a response and their forever-standing excuse. And they always manage to turn up the volume in their voice boxes to unthinkable decibels when they answer a phone call in public—an event that has rattled us all to the core at some point in our childhood. Those conversations, which are actually only expressing pure joy and excitement, to us as kids are the most mortifying moments our moms could put us through, and hence my inspiration for "When Hispanic Parents Talk on the Phone." You know what I'm talking about . . . the ever-increasing volume in her voice that those in her surrounding environment interpret as frantic yelling; the uncomfortable stares from other customers; the sheer embarrassment to us, who as Hispanic kids living in the United States get both sides of the story but would rather our parents keep it down and blend in a bit more; and the attempt to tell them that they're talking too loud only to be hushed to silence with a deathly glare and a whispered threat that leaves us cowering in a corner. We've all been there!

that if we really were fine, there would be no need to get defensive or upset about their questions. It is all for our greater good, even though in the moment all we want to do is lock ourselves in our rooms and never come out again.

The love and level of commitment our mothers have for our families is remarkable. When I look at all the sacrifices my mom has made for us, I am eternally grateful and inspired. Now that I'm older and able to analyze everything she's been through, I realize my mom is one of a kind. Especially when I compare her to other mothers. *What? Your mom doesn't call or text you every day to check in and see how you're doing? How does that work?* My mom and I are in touch on a daily basis, and she is and forever will be an intrinsic part of my life. So much so that when I started posting videos on Vine, even though I was already out of the house, technically an adult living on my own, I knew that whatever I posted was being closely scrutinized by my mom and I would get an earful if she found anything to be disrespectful or downright suspicious. Like the time I posted a Vine where the mom calls the daughter asking where she is, and the daughter replies, *"En casa de Yani fumando hookah,"* while playing with a lighter, to which the mom replies, *"¡Ay, señores, mi hija es drogadicta!"* immediately jumping to the conclusion that because she's smoking hookah her daughter is hooked on drugs. I'm talking about a six-second video, but as soon as I posted it, I got a call from my mom.

"Why do you have a lighter in your house? Are you smoking?"

"No, Mami, I use the lighter to light candles," I replied, honestly and somewhat annoyed.

But it's as if I had told her I used it to smoke pot. She honed in on that lighter and immediately imagined I was up to no good or at the very least hooked on cigarettes. What ensued was one of her infamous long-winded lectures about how terrible smoking is for my health and how it would affect every aspect of my life. After that, I quickly learned that whatever I posted would get the most critical review from none other than my own mother. She will always be on top of what I'm up to, and as annoying as that may be at times, I know it's because she is looking out for me no matter what. In fact, except for a few posts that may have been lost in translation, Mami and I are usually on the same page. I actually love that my videos are family-friendly and can have a positive impact on my viewers, regardless of how old or young they may be, or at the very least put a smile on their faces. To top it off, they usually brighten my mom's day too.

My mom has been so vocal throughout my life about the good and the bad, the do's and the don'ts, the rules, the commandments, the life lessons, the way we should present ourselves and act in public, that now her voice appears in my mind every time I'm brainstorming ideas for new videos. At the end of the day, my mom is not only one of my main sources of inspiration, she is also my moral compass.

# #DatingHispanicWomen

**I**T'S CHALLENGING; not everyone can do it. You are entering a fascinating, breathtaking, and oftentimes baffling realm. In order to navigate it to the best of your ability, you must decipher the language, the hidden messages, and the nonverbal cues. Only then will you have a fighting chance to date a Hispanic woman. But first you have to master the lost art of courtship, a challenge in itself, but one well worth the effort.

Hispanic women are not easy. Do not be confused by their sexy outfits and endless curves. If you want to date her, you are going to have to put in the work to get her attention. The thrill of the chase is real. It's all about your gestures and attention to detail. Make your courting style special, memorable, but not too over the top—if she senses you are desperate, that may be an immediate turnoff. You must do just enough for her to give you a second look and then linger to see what else you can bring to the table.

The Hispanic courting ritual is similar to those of birds you see on National Geographic—you know, the ones that fluff up their colorful feathers and perform a mating dance for the females in order to get their attention and, in our case, in order to get them to smile. So don't go buying her dozens of roses from the start, unless you know that's what she loves. Keep it simple. Listen to what she likes. If she says she loves chocolates, go to the store and get her a box. If she misses her mom's cooking, find a home-style restaurant with similar cuisine and suggest it as a first date. If she's into music, take her to see a live band. And do not expect anything in return. You might not be able to tell because she's good at playing coy, but she will notice every single detail and report back to her girlfriends. Hopefully, your charms have worked their magic and you've managed to make her swoon, *"Ay, qué chuloooo,"* rather than retch, "No he didn't, *¡qué cafre!"* If she's liking your moves, she may allow you to kiss her, but don't expect anything else until she is good and ready and sure you are worth her interest and time.

Okay, now let's say that you have managed to actually start dating a Hispanic woman: Be prepared to learn a new language. No, I'm not talking Spanish, I'm talking the language needed to date a Hispanic. First and foremost, be patient. Your girl is going to look amazing every time she walks out the door to meet you, but that takes work and time. Lots of time. She may take what seems like for-ev-er to get ready, but do not even think about rushing her through her makeup routine. It's just a recipe for disaster. "I am getting pretty for you, so I will let you know when I am ready to go. Understood?" Don't answer. Just walk away and let her do her thing. When she comes out the door, tell her how amazing she looks—it won't be hard because she is likely already stunning—and go off to enjoy your night. Believe me, the last thing you want is to get into a fight with your Hispanic girlfriend.

Eventually, it is going to happen. You will cross an invisible boundary, push a button you didn't even know existed, and you will piss her off for no apparent reason. However, the signs were all there, you just didn't know how to read them. The same non-verbal cues and signals that we are used to receiving from our parents when we are kids, those that we learn to interpret to know when we are crossing the point of no return, are also used by Hispanic women in relationships. I'm talking about that look they give you, with eyebrows quickly raised, when they don't like what someone just said; or the extra-tired look they send you, signaling they are ready to leave the party and go home. You are expected to pick up on all of these signs, and with time and observation, you will. But while you're learning the ropes, the inevitable will happen: you will piss off your girlfriend but be absolutely clueless about what you did wrong. All the warmth, joy, and love she usually displays will evaporate like water on a scorching hot day. And what is left will be a cold and standoffish shell of who she once was.

Puzzled, you dare to ask what's wrong: *"¿Qué te pasa?"*

*"Nada,"* she responds, burning a hole through your skin with her detached vibe.

*"Bueno, ¿qué quieres comer?"* you ask, innocently wanting to

change the subject and focus on where you're going to eat. Wrong move.

*"No tengo hambre,"* she replies. How could she be hungry if she's mad, is what she's really thinking, and why haven't you picked up on this yet!

*"Pero, mi amor,"* you continue insisting, now knowing something is up, but trying to see if not acknowledging it will make it go away, "tell me what you want to eat and I'll take you there."

*"Te dije que no tengo hambre,"* she says firmly, which is now code for "You have messed up big-time and if you continue to ignore the situation by asking me about food it will only get worse."

Yes, at this point you are in trouble. What to do? Where to begin? That's a difficult one. You could affectionately reach out to her and say, "You want to talk about it?" But you may be met with a *"¡No me toques! No quiero hablar contigo de nada."* Now you know, touching her is off-limits, and speaking to her must be done with absolute caution.

That's when the music comes in. If you're in the car, she will magically find the right song and blast it to make her point. Yes, by all means, pay attention to the lyrics and let her sing it out loud, in your face, to get her point across and let off some steam. In the meantime, retrace your latest steps, check the calendar, think about what you said. Did you offend her in any way? Did you not listen to her when she was trying to tell you about her day? Gasp, did you forget an important date? Valentine's Day? Anniversary? Birthday? Never, ever forget a date. Set up alarms in your calendar, do whatever it takes to avoid such a major mishap.

Family photo during our first trip to Walt Disney World in 1996. My mom always loved capturing those memories, even to this day.

My first bike! I got it for Christmas in 1998—man, I loved this thing.

Me and Papi at our home in Providence, Rhode Island, December 1990.

With my brother and best friend, Bryan. Ever since he was
little he's had dreams of one day becoming a pilot.

Escuela Elba Lugo Carrion school picture in Arecibo, Puerto Rico, May 2001. They always made us strike this pose!

Performing as Backstreet Boys at my sixth grade talent show in Escuela Elba Lugo Carrion, Arecibo, Puerto Rico, 2001.

Christmas when I was four years old at Plaza del Atlántico, posing with Santa Claus in Arecibo, Puerto Rico.

@LeMomJames with four-month-old me in her arms in Providence, Rhode Island, 1990, just before giving me a bath.

Mami and Papi, Christmas 1996, during our first trip to Walt Disney World.

Asking the love of my life to marry me when the clock struck midnight on
New Year's Eve in the presence of our family, January 1, 2019.

Me, Nahil, and baby Bryan, in December 1996, with our
*querida* Abuelita Carlita—her unconditional love, unwavering
support, and precious wisdom lives on forever in our hearts.

When the song is over, try to talk to her again, quietly, carefully. But don't start by asking if she's still mad, because if you do, you are in for a tirade.

*"Tú sabes bien lo que tú hiciste, ¡no te hagas el loco!"* she says, eyebrows furrowed and a finger flying in your face.

"Baby, I seriously don't know what I did, but I want to fix it."

*"Bájame el tonito de voz,"* she fires back, as if you're the one yelling at her.

By now, you just have to let it play out because she is not about to stand down. If she feels strongly about something, she will not let it go until she feels she has gotten her point across and has been heard. I remember seeing my dad in arguments with my mom and thinking he was too submissive with her: *When I have a girlfriend, I'm not going to be like that.* Yeah, right! You really don't get it until you are in the thick of it. When I first confronted these types of situations, I quickly realized there were two clear options:

1. I could fight a long and hard battle and possibly get my way in the end, but would have to deal with the aftermath of a grudge that would be held over my head for an unknown amount of time.
2. I could follow my dad's footsteps, give in, listen to her, do what she's asking of me, and keep the peace.

More often than not, I go with option number two. It's a much easier and quicker route out of the mess you are drowning in. *"Sí, mi amor. Está bien,"* agree and move on. Meanwhile, once you get to the bottom of her fury, make sure to take note and never make the same mistake again. Then bring on the peace and heal the battle wounds by showing her some love.

As hard as all of this may seem, you will likely reap the benefits of agreeing with your Hispanic girlfriend not only by preventing a fight, but also because she will always be looking out for you. Whatever decisions she makes will have your best interest at heart. She wants to see you succeed and be happy, because she loves being proud of you and showing you off to her friends and family. Oh, yeah, on that note, if you're dating a Hispanic woman, you will probably be meeting her entire family sooner than you'd expect. Go with the flow. If they like you, they will adopt you as their long-lost son, and you will be in for a treat.

Hispanic women are strong and dynamic. They will keep you on your toes, they will teach you lessons in love and care, they will shower you with affection, and challenge you with their points of view, and although at times it will be confusing, you will love every second of it. But if you cross them, if you break their hearts, if you—God forbid—cheat on them, then they will send you packing in the blink of an eye, because there are certain actions that are unforgivable.

If you ever try to break up with your Hispanic girlfriend, she will take the lead and break up with you first, saving you the trouble and herself the humiliation. But be prepared to feel her wrath. There will be no sobbing, there will be fire. You have now officially pushed her over the edge and unleashed the dragon, and she will burn you to the ground. If you came prepared for her tears, you have another thing coming. She will laugh in your face. She will curse you out: *"Mira, canto de estúpido, tú no sabes lo que te estás perdiendo."* She will put you in your place: *"Nunca nadie te va a tratar como yo, ¿oíste? Tú eres el que vas a sufrir porque yo no te necesito a ti."* She will enact worldwide revenge on you: *"Tú no eres nada, poco hombre, y me aseguraré de que se entere el mundo entero."* The entire world will know how small a man you really are, *¿te queda claro?* And she will tell you what you are going to die of: *"¡Ojalá cuando te estés bañando, te ahogues en el agua!"*

However, if the tables are turned and she really is the one initiating the breakup, then, brother, you are screwed. We may act tough, jealous, and dominant, but we know that our girlfriends are at the helms of our relationships, like all the dominant Hispanic female figures in our lives. The sooner you accept this, the better, because if you don't, you will likely get dumped, and losing your Hispanic girlfriend will feel like the end of the world; it will probably be the most torturous moment in your life. Your heart will be shattered and you will feel that you will never be able to recover from such pain and emptiness, but you will survive to live another day. And it may just bring you closer to the right one for you. If I hadn't gone through my share of breakups and heartbreaks, I wouldn't have been able to recognize the woman of my dreams, the one who would change my life and heart forever. And I also wouldn't have been prepared to cherish that relationship the way it deserves. Because each heartbreak was a key lesson in love and relationships. As the saying goes, *No hay mal que por bien no venga;* in other words, every cloud has a silver lining.

## Interpreting Hispanic Women

I am surrounded by women. I have been surrounded by women my entire life. My mom, my sister, my abuela, my tías, my primas, they have all been front and center at every family gathering and event. I have grown up listening to them talk, observing their mannerisms, paying attention to what bothers them and what makes them happy, deciphering what makes them tick. And even so, I think I've likely only scratched the surface, but I love them and take enormous pleasure in putting the little I do know about them in my videos. They are so nuanced that even the smallest gesture can differentiate a grandmother from a mother or a daughter. It's all in the details: the way they carry themselves, the words they use, the hand gestures, the eyes, the smirks and smiles. Just one quick roll of the eyes can let you know that I'm interpreting a daughter, while a quick pat of the hair can reveal it's an abuela.

I watch and observe my surroundings, process the information, and then try my best to imitate what I have seen. Imitating expressions is my thing, and I'm not afraid of my feminine side, a win-win when it comes to my videos. Women are amazing. Each movement of the hands and face allows me to instantly embody a different character, like in the "Baby Shower" video. It's a wonderful dynamic that I have seen play out in real life time and again. How the pregnant woman's words have an impact on the aunt, who turns to her daughter and says, "When are you going to give me a grandchild?" which is met with a gesture unleashing before our eyes a domino effect. I thrive on those delicate and intricate details and ultimately love that you as women can identify with these carefully selected interpretations. They are meant to make you laugh, but also to celebrate your awesomeness!

As complex as all this may sound on paper, the truth of the matter is that you would be so lucky to ever date a Hispanic woman. She is the most loving, caring, passionate, loyal, and reliable girlfriend you will ever have. If she loves you, she will love you hard. She will be there for you, helping you take cover during stormy weather and celebrating your light on sunny days.

The sky is blue, the grass is green, and women run our world. You women are powerhouses, you make things move, you make things right. The sooner we men accept this as a truth, the better off we will be in our relationships with not just our girlfriends and wives, but also our mothers, grandmothers, sisters, friends, and coworkers. We need you, we depend on you, and we can't live without you.

# #RelationshipGoals

ROMANCE IS EVERYWHERE in the Hispanic community. Big romantic gestures, drama, heartbreak, all-in love, you name it, we do it. It may be the novelas talking, or just our Latin roots, but passion is essential in our lives. We live, love, fight, and make up passionately. We celebrate love from the moment we are kids. In our imaginations, we're marrying off our friends' kids with our own, we go crazy when our toddlers hug or give each other a little peck. It's like the cutest thing ever for us, and there's always the family member who will start saying, *"¡Están enamorados!" "¡Ay, son noviecitos!"* "Oh, that's so cute!" Boys are taught to respect girls, and girls are taught to act like *señoritas* and demand respect. We're also taught to be kind, to treat people the way we want to be treated in every aspect of our lives, including relationships. It's not that we're handed a how-to book; it's everywhere we turn. All we have to do is sit, observe, and repeat what we see. And then put it into play.

My number one example when it comes to love and romance is my parents. I grew up seeing my father opening the car door for my mom and shutting it after she was safely seated, opening doors at restaurants and letting my mom go first, and behaving like the utmost respectful gentleman. I closely observed every loving and romantic gesture he made toward my mom, absorbed it, and when I reached my puppy love years, started to perfect my own romantic style as I searched for the love of my life.

When I think about the ideal couple, the one I look up to, the one I'd like to emulate as the years go by, I think of my parents. Their love story is the real deal. Mami and Papi met thirty-nine years ago, when they were only fifteen, in the Dominican Republic. It was 1982 and my dad was traveling from Camuy, his hometown in the northwest region of Puerto Rico, to Santo Domingo as a member of a basketball league to play against a Dominican team. It just so happened that my mom's brother was playing on the rival team that day. After the game, my dad and uncle hung out and became fast friends, and that's how, by casually introducing my father to his sister, my uncle made this unforeseen love connection a possibility.

Mami and Papi liked each other immediately, but my mom was studying to become a nun—straight out of a novela, right? However, her feelings for my dad were too strong to ignore, so she followed her heart and they eventually started dating. They were both in high school, in different countries, so what ensued was a long-distance relationship. For the following two years, my dad wrote my mom letters, saved up to call her on the phone, and pulled out all the stops to win her heart, including traveling to the Dominican Republic every chance he had just to see her. Remember, we're talking about a time when social media and e-mail didn't exist, when telephone calls were incredibly expensive, and snail mail took forever to reach its destination. But my dad wasn't about to give up. He got a job at a local *panadería* and worked in that bakery part-time throughout the school year just to save up enough money for his ticket to Santo Domingo.

As their relationship continued and became more serious, the families eventually traveled to meet each other. However, it seemed like it would be impossible to sustain such a love while carrying on different lives in different countries. My dad's family discouraged him from pursuing this relationship, urging him to end it and focus on his life in Puerto Rico, but my dad wasn't having it. The minute he turned eighteen, he traveled to Santo Domingo one last time and secretly asked my mom to marry him. She said yes, but on one condition: they wouldn't consummate the marriage until she was ready. As soon as she turned eighteen, that year, they left my mom's house, telling her family that they were off to the movies, and instead headed straight to the courthouse to elope. They consummated their marriage a month later, in part because my father respected my mother's wishes, and in part, I believe, because she wanted to prove to the world that their love was real and debunk the speculations that he only married her because she was pregnant: *"Oh, eso tiene que ser* that they're expecting," which was far from the truth. It was all for love.

Suffice to say neither of their families was pleased by their sudden and secret matrimony, but my mom's family accepted it and took my father in with open arms. All they ever wanted was to be together. After digesting the news, his family traveled to the Dominican Republic and planned their official wedding party, white dress and all. After a few months, my dad's mom convinced him to move back to Puerto Rico. At the time, it made sense. My dad would have a better shot at getting a job and providing for his bride in his hometown, so they said yes.

However, what followed wasn't easy. My mom went through hell and back. Puerto Rico and the Dominican Republic are brothers, but also big competitors. It's complicated. There is a lot of love and some hate too. Listen, if you're from either island, you know what I'm talking about. I love my *boricuas,* but some of them can be really tough on my Dominican brothers and sisters, with racist jokes and hard-line comments that go way back into the history of each of my beloved islands. I'm not about to give you a history lesson, just look it up if you're curious, or ask one of your Dominican or Puerto Rican friends. What I can tell you is that this history did not create a very friendly and welcoming environment for my mother. Many people passed judgment on her without even taking the time to get to know her. Had they done so, they would've quickly learned that she came from a well-off family, had a solid education, and was even on the road to getting a degree in accounting. She didn't need anything, she could've remained in Santo Domingo, but she moved for my father. She chose my dad over the comforts of her home—above all else, she chose love.

From the moment they said "I do," my mom and dad became inseparable. They faced the scrutiny together head-on, pushed forward, and persevered. My mom could've thrown in the towel at any given moment and said, "Forget this, I'm gone," but their bond was stronger than any trial or tribulation, and it has stood the test of time. They have created a life they are proud of and have three children who are the light in their eyes. After thirty-nine years together, married for thirty-four, they still consider each other best friends who are madly in love.

Their love story, their bond, their strength, that's what I have always aspired to create in my own relationship, and that's why I feel incredibly blessed to have found Camila, the love of my life, the person I want to grow old with, the woman who came into my world and made it and me better than I could've ever imagined.

It was a day like any other. Walking out of my local barbershop, I finally decided to check out the Tommy Hilfiger store that had opened a few weeks earlier. It was a good sign for that plaza off Highway 192, which had seen its heyday a few years earlier but had then hit a major slump. I had a soft spot for that place because it was the scene of my first job, at Nike. I walked into the new store and began browsing the racks, then casually looked up to my left and froze. There she was, standing at the register taking care of a customer, the most beautiful woman I had ever laid eyes on. I felt like one of those cartoons with my heart pounding outside my body, a reaction I had never experienced quite like this before. *What is going on?* I thought as I pressed my hand against my chest. In that instant, I knew I had to talk to her, but I didn't know how. *Wow, she's stunning.* My mind raced a mile a second trying to figure out how to get her attention. As extroverted as I may seem in my videos, I'm actually quite reserved in person. *Piropos* never fly out of my mouth. I've just never been that type of smooth operator. So there I was, staring at this gorgeous woman, absolutely dumbfounded and speechless. However, there was something inside that urged me to drum up the courage to say something, anything. Determined not to let this opportunity pass me by, I continued to stroll around the store, catching glimpses of her beauty and wondering how to break the ice and when. I figured I could kill a little more time until she was done with her customer, and that also bought me more time to come up with something clever to say. Distracted by these thoughts, mentally discarding options that I decided weren't good enough for her, I glanced in her direction one more time, but she was gone. I panicked. *Oh, no, I blew it!* Crushed, I turned my attention back to the rack I had been mindlessly browsing, and there she was, standing right next to me, like a divine apparition.

"Hey, do you need any help? Are you looking for anything in particular?" she asked.

This was my shot, this was my one chance at talking to her, but I froze. For a few seconds that felt like an eternity, I said absolutely nothing and then became a blubbering, stuttering mess and managed to reply, "Nah, I'm just here waiting for a friend." What the hell was I thinking? What friend? There was no friend coming!

"Okay, let me know if you need anything else," she said politely and walked away.

Done. I bombed. It was awful. I'd completely botched my one chance to speak to this striking woman. Now what? I had told her I was waiting for someone, so I couldn't go up to her to make conversation, and I couldn't exactly leave either. *How long should I wait so that she doesn't realize I just made that up?* I was clueless, so I lingered a little while longer, until I lost sight of her and hightailed it out of there.

On my way home, I couldn't get this girl out of my mind. She was a vision. I wondered if we had any friends in common. Kissimmee is a small area, with just a few schools, so the chances of finding a common connection with someone you don't know are pretty high. The following day, I woke up thinking of her and realized I only had one option left: I had to work on a better opener and head back to the store. Determined to make a better impression, I let a few days go by and went back in, but she was nowhere to be found. She probably wasn't working that day, so I had to try my luck again. However, if I started hanging out at the store every day, I'd look like a plain old stalker, and that was not the message I wanted to send, so I devised another plan. I began to get more haircuts. That was the perfect excuse. I'd freshen up my style and casually walk into the store as if I hadn't spent the whole week planning that moment.

A couple of weeks went by, but I kept missing her. My barber noticed something was up and said, "Wow, you're coming a lot more lately."

"Yeah, yeah, I just want to make sure I look fresh," I replied, casually. I wasn't about to confess I was love-struck and hoping God would give me a second shot at speaking to the woman I couldn't get out of my mind.

Needless to say, I spent a lot of money at the barbershop that month, but it was the best investment I have ever made because, at long last, the day arrived. I walked into the shop and there she was. My heart skipped a beat and then began racing like a Formula 1 car on the track. *Pull it together, Juan. Come on, it's now or never. Don't blow it again.* As I approached her, I noticed she was under the weather, but this time I brought my A game.

I started with a casual "Hey, how are you?" and she said hi back. Good start, so I kept going. "Not sure if you remember me from the other day." And to my surprise she replied, "Yeah, are you waiting for a friend again?" Wait, she was gorgeous and funny? I was on a roll now—at least we were actually chatting, and I even managed to make her laugh. Success! As we continued talking, she mentioned the days she worked at the store, and we eventually exchanged numbers. I couldn't believe my luck!

When I got home that afternoon, I was over the moon with excitement, but I decided to play it cool and text her the following day—something she brought up later, puzzled, because she knew I'd liked her all along. All I know is that it worked. I started to show up at the store more often on the days she worked and we slowly built a good rapport. I had to be careful, I didn't want to screw this up. I had recently quit my job to pursue my social media career full-time but was floating in limbo, trying to figure out my next steps, so I had a lot of time on my hands—time I decided to focus on her. I wanted to show her my interest while also going out of my way to be a gentleman. I listened to her carefully, picked up on her likes and dislikes, and began showing up on her lunch break with flowers, food, love notes, and other small gestures that set me apart and made her smile. Even though I wasn't quite sure how she felt about me, I wanted to show her that I was serious. She didn't make it easy, she kept me on my toes, but I got a thrill from the chase and the unknown, and I think the romance skills I had picked up from my dad finally paid off.

As more days passed, we spent so much time together and shared so much that we slowly became inseparable. If she wasn't working or at school, we were together. Anytime I knew she was free, I'd be right there waiting for her. One day, while chatting, we came to find out that she had lived in Poinciana around the same time I did, and only four blocks away! We were so amazed and surprised that our paths hadn't crossed sooner. But things have a way of working out on their own. *El tiempo de Dios es perfecto.*

Meanwhile, I kept our budding friendship and possible relationship close to my chest. But my mom knew something was different, as all moms do. And as all Hispanic moms do, she had to get to the bottom of why I had suddenly fallen off the map, *"Oye, ¿y con quién tú andas que no vienes tanto para la casa?"* That was it, I had no choice but to fess up about why I'd been blind to the rest of the world lately. "I met this girl"—doesn't it always start off like that? I filled both my parents in. "Her name is Camila," I said, and pulled out my phone to show them pictures. I confessed that I was really serious and invested in her, which led to the meeting of the parents. Fortunately, my parents loved her, and her mom loved me, so all was set for my next move. I gathered the courage to ask Camila if she would like to join me on my upcoming work trip to New York. She'd never been, so I figured it would be a chance not only for us to go on our first little trip together, but also for her to see that fantastic city. She accepted, and I was thrilled. Now I would be able to carry through with the following piece of this traveling puzzle, which I had carefully thought through.

We were staying in New Jersey, so once we arrived and settled in, we hopped on a bus into the city and went straight to Times Square. It was really cold that day. As we stood in that sweet spot looking up at all the billboards and lights, I turned to Camila, hugged her with one arm as I positioned my phone in my free hand, and then asked her, "Do you want to be my girlfriend?" to which she replied a resounding "Yes!" I couldn't have been happier. I already knew this was the woman of my dreams, and now she had confirmed that she was just as serious about me as I was about her.

When we got back to Orlando, committed to one another and ready to see where our lives would take us, I was still in the early stages of my social media career, struggling to make ends meet, but Camila was there for me every step of the way. She helped me with my phone bill and other expenses when I was strapped for cash while always making me feel that we were a team, together through thick and thin in everything. A few times, she even helped me with my rent. I was astounded at how invested in and supportive of my dreams she was, and how much she believed in me, especially when my confidence wavered and I wondered if I should follow another path.

Meanwhile, she was in college, working, still living at home, and at a crossroads in her life that was begging for a change. Even though many people thought it was too soon, that we were moving too fast, around seven months into our relationship, we decided to take a leap of faith and move in together. Camila's mom was pretty accepting of our decision. She liked me and was at ease knowing that I was 100 percent invested in her daughter. Additionally, she knew it was time for her daughter to fly the nest and experience something new, like living with someone other than her mom. When I told my folks, they questioned our decision and told me there was no need to rush, but in the end, knowing and loving Camila, they were cool with it too. However, my mom added, "With one condition: if you want to live with a girl," she said, "you have to make some changes in here. This is a bachelor's pad and not fit for a woman." As I looked around and saw my sneakers on the floor and the LeBron James posters on the walls, I realized she was right. My place needed a makeover. As soon as I received my tax refund, it went straight to redecorating my apartment to give Camila the welcome she deserved. I painted the walls, bought a proper couch, and made it cozy enough so that when she walked in, she would feel it was an actual and livable home. And it worked.

When Camila and I moved in together, it felt like it was meant to be. Neither of us was a party animal, so we both enjoyed staying home and watching movies. We liked each other's

## Hispanic Pressure: Marriage and Kids—ASAP!

Camila and I lived together for five years without taking the next step in our relationship, and that drove our families, friends, and followers completely bonkers. *"¿Y, qué están esperando?"* We were constantly flooded with questions about when we were going to get hitched and have babies. It's just part of our Hispanic DNA, I know, but what's the rush? And yes, I'm going to sound more American than Hispanic, but, really, why can't we just enjoy our twenties and establish ourselves as adults before taking on even bigger responsibilities like marriage and kids? It's not like we never talked about this. Camila and I have always been on the same page, which to us meant checking the marriage and baby madness at the door and really enjoying our relationship. We knew we would take the next step when we were both good and ready . . . and that's why, five years later, we are at long last engaged—and our families couldn't be happier! Now, please, calm down, don't start hounding us to set a date and pop out babies. Like everything we've done up until now, we want to savor this moment. After all, it's a once-in-a-lifetime experience—one of many more to come, because anything I do with Camila by my side is an absolute blessing and a dream come true . . .

company, shared everything, and really considered each other best friends. However—and if you've ever moved in with anyone, you know there is going to be a *however*—although we got along superbly, like any other couple, we faced growing pains. All change requires adjustment and compromise, which was definitely a huge learning curve for us. That's when it got real, when our patience was tested, when our first real fights emerged. That's when you truly get to see the good, the bad, and the ugly. That's when I had to put everything I knew about dating a Hispanic woman into effect. Go with the flow, read the nonverbal cues, and do not question why something has to be cleaned or put away a certain way, or why it bothered her so much if I didn't follow through with that. It just is what it is. Those are not battles worth fighting.

Hey, I was no walk in the park either. It took me some time to change my bachelor-pad ways and realize that now I was sharing my space with someone else, a woman no less, and I could no longer do whatever floated my boat. My individual decisions and actions at home were now affecting Camila too, and I had to accept this fact. At first, it wasn't easy. After all, as much as I tried to control it, I did inherit my mom's hot temper. However, I quickly realized that this wasn't my mom I was dealing with. I couldn't fight with Camila and shut her out of my life by going to my room, because now that room was shared with her. I hated those sleepless nights after our first fights, the air hovering above our bed thick with negativity and pleading for reconciliation.

Yet there was one outstanding element that helped us navigate those murky waters of coexisting under the same roof: communication. When something bothered us, when we got into arguments, eventually we were able to talk things out and cross those hurdles together. Sure, she'd call me out if I lagged in my gentlemanly manners, but that helped me realize that consistency in a relationship is essential. So, if your girlfriend, fiancée, or wife is used to having doors opened or getting flowers, then keep it up, because she'll notice if you don't. Listen, I'm still learning, but I have a fantastic coach by my side lighting the way.

Fortunately, all of this happened at a time in my life when I understood that relationships are amazing, but they also take work and sacrifice. I was so tired of trying to find love in all the wrong spots, meeting a woman and then being disappointed by yet another something that went nowhere, that when I discovered this precious gem before me, I was ready to do everything in my power to make it work with her. And she made it easy.

I say this all the time, if it weren't for Camila, I don't think I would be where I am today. I was doing okay when I met her, but she pushed me to the next level. She's proactive and a go-getter, and her energy constantly drives me to reach for the stars. Everyone sees what's in front of the camera, but no one gets to see the real behind-the-scenes. Camila will sit with me for an entire day and help me brainstorm and develop a solid concept for a video. Once we've nailed the idea, she suggests outfits, and she is the person behind the camera shooting every scene while I'm acting.

The beauty of our relationship is that we push each other to rise to every occasion, because we each want the other to succeed and be happy and be the best at whatever we set our minds to. That's why, when I finally hit my stride financially, Camila and I decided that it was time for her to quit her job and pursue her dreams. I was at a place where I could take care of both of us for a while, so I suggested she use this time to focus on her college degree full-time. I know accepting this proposal wasn't easy for her. It's never easy for any of us to depend on someone else once we've left our parents' home; it makes us feel extremely vulnerable. What if you give up your income and the other person suddenly leaves you? There are risks to weigh, but once again, she took a leap of faith, and finished her degree with flying colors.

A big part of life is love. The love between parents and their children, the love between relatives, the love between friends, and romantic love. They are all essential pieces of our existence in this world. The minute I saw Camila, I came full circle with love. I knew I wanted her by my side for the rest of my days. Throughout these first five years of our journey together, she has seen my struggles and triumphs, my insecurities and accomplishments. She's calmed me down and lifted me up, and has stuck with me through the ups and downs as my steadfast partner and best friend. Camila is the love of my life. I thank God for such an immense blessing, and I thank her for choosing to be by my side. I only hope I can make her even half as happy as she makes me.

# #Abuela

THE GRANDMOTHER, or abuela, as we call this magnanimous figure in our lives, is the heart of the Hispanic family. She has the ability to make us feel like she can protect us from everything that is happening outside. She's our safety blanket, comforting us and keeping us from harm's way. She is also the family member most sought out for her advice, for her profound wisdom, for those words we know will stay with us through the rest of our lives—and for her food. She understands our concerns, perspectives, and needs, and does her best to listen empathetically as we pour our hearts out to her generous soul, while feeding us our favorite treats.

Abuela Carlita, my mom's mom, was our very own majestic wizard, wise beyond her many years. My mom, my dad, my sister, my brother, and I would all turn to her first when we were perplexed by our circumstances, when we were sad and lost, and when we had accomplishments that were worth celebrating, because she was always there for us. Unconditionally loving, heartwarming, enlightened, and kind, Abuela Carlita was an unwavering member of our family, our rock.

Like most Hispanic grandmothers, my abuela was the glue that held our family together, the peacekeeper. She always tried to talk sense into her children and grandchildren, urging us to take a step back and put ourselves in the other person's shoes to reach an agreement and, ultimately, reconciliation. And when it came to *pelas*, she was my very own superhero. The minute my mom came charging after me for misbehaving in some shape or form, Abuela Carlita would nosedive between us, intervening in my favor by trying to talk some sense into my mom. While I shut my eyes and prayed to God, I'd hear her say, *"Déjenlo quieto, no le den, que él es un niño bueno. Él se va a portar bien."* And then my mom would take a deep breath and lower her arm, respecting her mom's wishes and sparing me a *chancletazo*. Abuela Carlita had been there, done that; it was likely that she saw the entire scene from a fresh and wiser perspective, or maybe the years had made her more docile, or maybe she simply had a soft spot for her grandchildren. Whatever it was, I was always eternally grateful.

This doesn't mean our abuelas won't scold us when needed. They have full permission from our parents to discipline us as they see fit, but their methods are lighter and usually come in the form of a verbal reprimand followed by an explanation: *"Pero mi niño, tú sabes que yo te quiero y quiero lo mejor para ti, pero te tienes que comportar, mi amor."* And with that, somehow we feel they understand us more than our parents ever will. That's also why we hardly get into fights with our abuelas. How could we? They are the epitomes of kindness and love, always spoiling us rotten when our parents aren't looking and consoling us with their magical delicacies to help cheer us up when we are down. Because my abuela's *sancocho* is better than yours! That's what we all think and will continue to believe till the day we die.

Our abuelas are the five-star chefs in our families. They have that secret touch, the secret ingredient, and they take pride in their cooking and our devouring every last bite. They know each family member's favorite dish and rejoice when they have a chance to make it for us. That moment when our abuela serves us a massive plate of food and places it before us is absolutely priceless. The happiness on her face— *"Te hice la carnecita de res que te gusta con habichuelas y arroz"*; the anticipation of our first bite— *"¿Te gustó la comida?"*; and the hope that we will shower her with compliments— *"Sí, Abuela, está buenísimo"*— that's all she needs to hear. As soon as we are done with our food, she seizes our plates and, while serving a second helping, asks, *"¿Quieres un poquito más, mi niño?"* Unable to crush her need to feed us, we give in and say yes and immediately enter food coma territory as we wolf down more of her feast into already overcrowded stomachs. But it's all worth it for her. It's a ritual that begs to be passed down from generation to generation, because it is made of pure and unconditional love.

Once she believed that we were well fed and taken care of, my abuela would quickly clean up and dash over to her coveted spot on the couch to watch her nightly can't-miss novela, *"Es que se está poniendo bien buena, mijo."* What is it about our abuelas and moms and their novelas? I never got the over-the-top, intense dramatics of these shows, but they gobble them up like addicts. I have fun thinking back on these times and making fun of them in my videos because I hated novelas and their incredibly predictable story lines.

"Is this really what you guys are watching?" I'd exclaim, in the hope that they might for once concede and change the channel.

*"¡Ay Dios mío, es que no se ha dado cuenta que ese es su hijo!"* they'd reply with excitement and impatience, waving me away.

"Wait, what? How could she not know that's her son, it's so obvious!"

But it was like talking to a wall. I was immediately and completely ignored. Bringing my mother and grandmother down to reality defied the purpose of this magic hour. Those characters were now part of their circle of friends. They were so invested in the accomplishments and failures of the novela characters' lives that they detested the bad guys with a vengeance, felt terrible pity for the dumb ones, and fervently rooted for the good ones as if they were part of their own family.

"Come on, Abuela, it's not real. Mami, really?" I'd interject, just to rile them up.

"Shht, *cállate*—move over and keep quiet," they'd respond, almost in unison.

Let's face it. This is preestablished in the Hispanic home as such a sacred and uninterruptible time that if we dare cut in, our moms and grandmothers will shut us down without even flinching away from the screen. The DO NOT DISTURB sign is up. This is their me-time, a break from the reality of their day-to-day responsibilities. As Hispanic kids, we grow up learning to respect our elders and to never dare infringe upon our abuelas' and mothers' sacred hour of love, lust, and heart-wrenching tears, no matter how silly it seems to our Americanized eyes.

The importance of these novelas goes beyond pure entertainment; they are topics of conversation in the community, among friends and family. If you want to be part of the inner circle, you'd better know what happened last night in the novela between Aurelio and María. The story lines become the main theme at work, at the hair salon, online, or in any other Hispanic social setting, together with another biggie in our community: *las noticias.*

Hispanics generally take great pride in knowing what is going on at home and abroad. They never shy away from a conversation involving local and international issues. On the contrary, they're ready and eagerly waiting to chime in with their commentary, which they picked up on TV the night before. Their source of information is the six o'clock news, humming in the background while they start making dinner, or the eleven o'clock news—right after the novelas, of course! My abuela especially loved Univision's news program *Primer Impacto*, which airs at 5:00 p.m., the perfect time slot for a little *cafecito* break before heading into the kitchen to cook. That's why when I first appeared on that show, after she had passed away, I silently dedicated it to her, knowing how excited she would've been to see me there.

Each one of these programs keeps our abuelas up-to-date with the must-know information to later be discussed with family and friends. Because watching *las noticias* is not just about staying informed, it is also a big source of entertainment and part of their socialization.

"Oh, did you hear about the latest protest in Venezuela?"

*"Ay, sí, bendito, pobre gente."*

*"Sí, las cosas están malas. Hay que rezar."*

The news allows our families to empathize with their friends on the gravity of the situations in their countries and offer a helping hand or a prayer in their friends' time of need. It also allows them to stay connected to their family members back home, so they can talk politics on the phone while catching up and find out how the latest issues are affecting their loved ones. Because, as Hispanics, we don't only want to know how you're doing, we want to make sure your parents, siblings, grandparents, aunts, uncles, and cousins are all okay too. It's a family affair through and through. What I always find amusing is that when these topics come up, the worse the situation is, the better and juicier the conversation.

*"Hola, tía, how are things down there? I heard inflation is up."*

*"Ay, sí, mija, ya tú sabes, las cosas están malas. Este presidente no sabe lo que hace."*

Yes, we love to exaggerate, likely influenced by all the novelas we have been watching throughout generations. Drama is part of our everyday life, but so is our tenacious optimism, because regardless of what we may be facing, we put our faith in God that it is happening for a reason and eventually things will start looking up. *Dios sabe lo que hace.* So when my abuela read the obituaries in the newspaper, she didn't feel bad for the friend or acquaintance who had passed away, because now he or she was with God, but she did feel sorry for those left behind. I was sometimes puzzled by my grandparents' fascination with the obituaries, but then realized that it also served a purpose. It allowed them to send notes to the suffering families, stop by the wakes with a plate of food to pay their respects, or cheer up their grieving friends at the local salon or barbershop. Because as gossipy and *bochincheras* as our grandmothers, mothers, and aunts may be, they have each other's backs.

Given that novelas and news and entertainment programs are such vital parts of our abuelas' daily communication with others, the TV after dinner belongs to them. So, if you happen to walk by the living room and see your abuela dozing in front of the screen, do not, for the life of you, turn that TV off. I have made this mistake, only to stir my abuela awake as soon as I pressed the off button and receive an angry and somewhat embarrassed glare from her half-asleep eyes.

*"Pero, Abuela, tú estabas durmiendo,"* I'd say apologetically, letting her know that she had fallen asleep.

*"Noooo, ¿yo? Yo no estaba durmiendo. ¿Tú estás loco?"* she'd answer defensively, not wanting to admit that she'd dozed off and been incapable of giving up the remote because she wanted so much to catch one last glimpse of her forever crush, Don Francisco, before officially going to bed.

I cherish each and every one of these memories and can recall them as if they happened yesterday because I loved spending time with my grandparents. Finding out that my parents were taking me to my grandparents' for a weekend sleepover was getting the best news of the week when I was a kid. I knew that meant eating my favorite food and staying up a little later than usual watching TV. Being grandparents is like knowing they've gotten a second chance at righting the wrongs they made with their own children, and they go all out in the process. Pleasing and spoiling us are among the things that make our grandparents happiest—hey, I'm not one to complain about this! To top it off, many of those weekends ended with a long-standing ritual—a top-secret transaction between abuela and grandchild that takes place as we say our goodbyes. It comes right between the hug and the kiss, a ten- or twenty-dollar bill is slipped into your hand or pocket with whispered advice asking you to behave with your parents, *"Necesito que te portes bien. Hazle caso a tu padre y tu madre,"* followed by a complicit *"No le digas a tu mamá que te di este dinero. Cómprate algo que te guste,"* urging you to keep the money you just clandestinely received to yourself so you can buy something you want. Spoiling to the tenth degree, something only our abuelas can get away with.

Abuela Carlita stopped everything to be with us. She sold her business and property, uprooted her life and her husband, and moved from the Dominican Republic to Puerto Rico as soon as she realized my mom was struggling and needed her help. She was there when my mom had my sister. She and my abuelo were there in Rhode Island when I was born. They were there for my little brother's birth, and they were there in each and every move we made after that between Puerto Rico and Orlando. My memories of my grandparents really kick in during our first stint in Orlando. At the time, they had moved in with my uncle, whose home served as our after-school getaway. My parents would drop us off at school before heading to work, and when our school day was over, the bus would leave us at my grandparents' place.

## The "Havana" Video

When Camila Cabello approached me, asking me to be a part of her music video, at first I hesitated. I'd been offered cameos before, but had passed them up because I didn't feel they added much to the projects. But Camila's offer was different: she wanted me to interpret the abuela. It was a chance to do something interesting that would actually resonate with my audience, while playing a role inspired by my abuela Carlita. So after some thought, I said yes. I had worked on sets for commercial shoots before, but never a full-on video shoot with a movie feel like that one. It was a little intimidating at first, but as soon as I heard the word "action," all stage fright went out the window and I was in the zone, channeling my abuela's gestures and words into this character. I had a great time, although filming that very last scene, where I'm dancing, was a little embarrassing. There I was in my abuela getup, grabbing the broom, trying to do my thing in a room full of men yelling out, "I need you to act more feminine. I need you to act like a girl." And then, I suddenly clicked into character and went all in, grabbing that broom as if it were my star-crossed lover, and dancing around the kitchen like I had seen my abuela do so many times. It was so much fun. I only wish Abuela Carlita could've seen it.

That's where Abuela Carlita would kick into high gear, offering us snacks, helping us with our homework, making us take showers, so we were fresh, clean, and ready to be picked up by my parents after their long day at work.

For my sister, my brother, and me, she was more than a grandmother, she was really like a second mother. My father felt the same way. She took him under her wing when he faced issues with his own family and remained by his side through all the ups and downs, watching and nurturing him as he went from an eighteen-year-old boy to a forty-some-year-old man. He will never forget her generosity of spirit and kindness. When he talks about her, it is with pure love, remembering her fondly and missing her presence to this day.

I understand where my dad is coming from. Abuela Carlita was truly one of a kind. During my rebellious streak, when I was struggling with my parents, she always took the time to sit me down and say, "Don't worry, you're a kid, you're going to be all right. Try to be good to your parents." She knew I didn't mean any harm, she could see it all from her perspective, and it was refreshing and a relief for me as a misunderstood teenager to find that support at home. She was also my steadfast supporter, always cheering me on when I participated in school talent shows, dancing and singing Backstreet Boys tunes, and my number one fan when I messed around with our video recorders, shooting short videos and directing my family in my mini movies just because I thought it was fun.

Never did I once think that I would make a career out of this, but somehow Abuela Carlita knew my artistic inclinations would amount to more than I ever dreamed of. *"¡Tú tienes mucho talento!"* she'd exclaim often to encourage me to pursue a talent I thought she only saw through her love-tinted glasses. Now, when I recall those moments, I get goose bumps. It was as if she had some sort of premonition. Or maybe it was part of her unconditional love and support toward her grandchildren. She always inspired my little brother to follow his passion and become a pilot. And she did the same with my sister, filling her with encouragement to pursue her dreams. That's why Nahil dedicated her PhD in psychology to Abuela Carlita. I only wish Abuela could see her today. My sister is an example in our family. The first one to get a doctorate, as an immigrant and a Hispanic woman no less, she has surpassed her share of roadblocks and pursued her passion to help people with mental health problems. Nahil is pure inspiration, and I know Abuela would be as proud of her as I am of everything she has accomplished and looking forward to all that's still to come.

Abuela Carlita, like many abuelas in Hispanic homes, was our gem, a fundamental part of our lives. So when she started getting sick, rather than put her in an old folks' home, we did everything in our power to keep her close and alive. Because Hispanic families never turn their backs on their grandparents. When our abuelas and abuelos get old and can no longer care for themselves, we move them in with us, no questions asked, unless their health is so deteriorated that they actually need 24-7 care. I live across the street from a nursing home and often see the *viejitos* living there, and it breaks my heart. This option doesn't even cross our minds, not only because our grandparents are so beloved, but because after sacrificing themselves to give us all a better life, they deserve the best when their time is coming to an end. We want them to be surrounded by their loved ones; we want to make them laugh. It's part of the cycle of our lives; we want to be able to take care of them the way they took care of us as kids, which is what we did with my abuela.

Unfortunately, Abuela Carlita passed away five years ago, but she is still very much alive and present in our hearts and memories. She was the kindest and most beautiful person I have ever met. She never had a bad thing to say about others. She was always smiling, always positive, and always urging us to pray, to seek God, and to treat others the way we would like to be treated.

I still feel Abuela Carlita's presence; I feel she's up above, protecting me, and smiling that wonderful smile from heaven. Everything that has happened in my life since her passing, how it's all transpired, my budding social media career, is a true gift from God and my abuela. I know she would be so proud of all of my accomplishments if she were still here with us. I would do anything to be able to speak with her and hug her one more time, but I take comfort in carrying her voice within me—*Tú vas a ser famoso*—and thanking her in each one of my prayers. Thank you for believing in me, Abuela Carlita.

# #TheHouse

I N 2011, ABUELA CARLITA was diagnosed with brain cancer, a moment that became a catalyst for change in all our lives. My mom's mom meant the world to us. She was our rock, our gem, the beloved heart of our family. So when she got cancer, my parents were determined to do absolutely everything in their power to keep her alive.

Right before her diagnosis, my parents were doing quite well for themselves. They had been able to leave their grueling jobs behind and become small business owners in Orlando and Puerto Rico. Before the 2008 housing crisis, they were in a steady enough financial situation to buy not one but two homes in Poinciana. We called the first one on Robin Lane home until they purchased the second one, which was big enough to also house my grandparents. Then, the economic crisis hit full force. Loans started to fluctuate, fixed interest rates disappeared, their mortgages went up, and everyone started spending less, which to my parents meant suddenly limited resources and income. As if that weren't nerve-racking enough, my grandmother's brain cancer reared its ugly head. Now my parents' sole mission in life was to get her the treatment she needed.

After seeking several medical opinions, my parents were referred to a specialist, the one place they thought my grandmother would have a fighting chance. But this doctor was far away from home, in our old stomping grounds: Rhode Island. In a desperate move, my parents decided to rent an apartment up there and split their lives between Rhode Island and Orlando. They checked my grandmother in to a clinic and, for the following year, stayed in Orlando during the week to take care of their businesses and returned to Rhode Island every weekend to be by her side.

Meanwhile, given the economic crisis and the great financial toll this new plan was taking, my parents lost their larger house to foreclosure and moved into the smaller one. By then, my sister and I were attending college and had already moved out, but my brother was still in school, so that year he spent his summer vacation in Rhode Island with my parents and grandmother.

After months of flying back and forth, trying to keep their businesses afloat while maintaining two homes and dealing with the pile of medical bills accumulating on their dining room table, my parents' circumstances began to eat them alive. But they powered through, determined to save my grandmother's life. By then, they could no longer keep up with the mortgage payments on their remaining home, and they lost it too. In just a couple of years, they had gone from thriving owners of not one but two houses to none, and my abuela wasn't showing any clear signs of recovery. It was absolutely heartbreaking.

Then came the dreaded words from Abuela Carlita's Rhode Island doctor, the sentence no family ever wants to hear: "There's nothing else we can do for her." With that, my parents packed up their belongings and moved Abuela back to Orlando, with only prayers for a miracle cure, prayers my mom and dad said every day from the moment she was diagnosed to her last breath.

Abuela Carlita's health had deteriorated so much that they had to put her in hospice care, the absolute last resort, but there really was no other option. Spending what little money they had left, my parents chose a place nearby, so they could be with my grandmother every single day and accompany her with their unconditional love and support until the end.

By this time, I had stopped visiting her. I adored Abuela Carlita so much that I couldn't handle seeing her in such a dilapidated state. I stood strong by my parents' side, but made the difficult and conscious choice to preserve the memory of my abuela in full bloom, rather than the wilting flower that brain cancer had turned her into. Even though I knew her death was imminent, on December 14, 2013, when she passed away, I was heartbroken. She was not only my beloved abuelita, but also the first person close to me to die. Although I knew she was now in a better place, coming to terms with the fact that I would never see her or talk to her again or hear her laughter and advice shook me to the core and really brought home the finality of death.

My parents were left in dire financial and emotional straits, but they wouldn't have had it any other way. If you ask my mom, she'll tell you she doesn't regret any of those decisions; she lives at peace, knowing she did everything in her power to breathe a few last breaths into her mother's life. Hispanic children will climb the highest hills and move the biggest mountains for our mothers, whatever it takes, because the love of a child for his or her mother is irreplaceable.

Losing their houses was one of the biggest disappointments in my parents' lives. After all the fourteen-hour workdays, the exhaustion, the penny-pinching and saving, they were left with nothing but an enormous uphill financial struggle as they reached their fifties. Furthermore, those foreclosures killed their credit scores, which made it practically impossible to dream of buying another house because no bank wanted to touch them. It felt like there really was no light at the end of the tunnel, but they still held their heads up high and put their best foot forward, making do with what they did have, and knowing that they would do it all over again if it meant giving Abuela Carlita a few more days in this world. Plus, they had managed to raise three healthy and strong children and still had each other, so all was not lost in their eyes.

As I observed these unforeseen and difficult circumstances through my newly formed adult eyes, I knew I had to do something. Growing up, I honestly felt like I had everything I ever needed. If I wanted to go to the park, I could go; if I wanted to go to a baseball game, my parents would take me. We always had presents under the Christmas tree, food on the table, and clothes on our backs. Mami and Papi gave my siblings and me everything they could afford while also keeping us humble, teaching us that the small luxuries we had were due to endless hard work. They were my ultimate superheroes, working two jobs each, keeping us safe, feeding us, looking after us, and never skipping a beat in the process.

When I think about everything my parents did for us, I sometimes wonder if I would ever be capable of such sacrifice. Now that I am out in the world, I have a clearer understanding of just how arduous and challenging their lives were, and I appreciate it more than ever before. Humbled and eternally grateful, after all they have done to raise us and give us all the tools we need to succeed, I just couldn't stand on the sidelines anymore and watch them continue to struggle.

I needed to do something to repair this situation for my parents. God had given me a career and the opportunity to finally give them the home they deserved, a place where we could create new memories. I had always dreamed of that moment, of being able to buy them a home, of lifting the burden of rent and mortgage payments, of giving them a place to call their own, debt-free. However, having lived and learned through my parents' own experience, I knew clearly that before making such a big investment, I had to make sure my own finances were solid enough. I didn't want something like their foreclosures to ever happen to us again. After saving and making sure my resources could handle it, I took the plunge and made our dreams come true.

Walking down the street, with my mom to my right and my dad to my left, both blindfolded and following my lead to a surprise they had no idea was coming, I felt my heart was going to explode. The time to at long last give back and thank my parents for the many sacrifices they had endured to take care of all of us had arrived. I watched as they slipped off their blindfolds at my cue and stared at the house before them completely awestruck, for a brief moment unable to move or react. Tears started rolling down my mom's face as I approached my parents, sobbing, and said, *"Tu casa nueva, Mami. Papi, esta es tu casa."* This is your home. We embraced in a long hug and cried together, overwhelmed by love and forever grateful for this blessing. As we slowly walked to their new home, they thanked me profusely. I told them what amazing parents they were and how they deserved this and so much more. "Now it's our turn to take care of you," I added.

My parents are my inspiration, they are my life, they are the people who pushed through their darkest hours to give us a better life, and it was time to thank them for all those years of hard work and toil. This was not only a son's dream come true, or simply my way of saying thank you for everything they did for us as a family; this was not just the American Dream in full force. We had finally come full circle. They had lost their homes trying to save Abuela Carlita's life, and now their son was giving them a new beginning with the house of their dreams. And that's why I dedicated this amazing moment "In Loving Memory of Carlita Ortiz," because I know my grandmother would've suffered if she'd known that my parents had lost both their homes trying to save her. But I also know that now she is up in heaven smiling down on us, because God made them travel down that desolate path only to reward them with an even better house. God is good.

I still don't think Mami and Papi understand what an enormous role they have played in my life and career. The lessons and experiences that have shaped me are in large part due to them. Thanking them with a house was the least I could do, and it was a gift for me too. My happiness comes from seeing my loved ones happy. If my mom, dad, brother, sister, and fiancée are okay, then I'm okay, because they are my driving forces and the people that make my life worth living.

# #BecomingLeJuanJames

**I**'VE ALWAYS BEEN reserved. I know, shocking, right? Most people who see my videos immediately assume I'm this extroverted, energetic, life-of-the-party kind of guy, but that's LeJuan James, my alter ego. When it comes to Juan Atiles, it's a different story. I'm not shy, I'm basically the mellow observer. Home is my happy place, and that's where my creativity flourishes. I tap into my surroundings, quietly sitting back to watch and learn from my family and friends in action, or sometimes even passersby in the neighborhood. I latch on to things that ring true to me, jog a poignant memory to the surface, or simply make me laugh, and I run with them. This is how it's always been.

As a kid, I would hang out with my cousins during the weekend or over the summer and come home speaking like them. I'd pick up on their vocabulary, their accents, their gestures.

My mom would look at me and laugh, instantly recognizing what family member I was imitating by the way I talked, my tone, my mannerisms. What neither she nor I even realized at the time was that I was practicing impersonations that would later pop up in my videos for the world to see. It came naturally to me. I love trying to imitate accents from different countries, and since I was always surrounded by Dominicans and Puerto Ricans, I was able to dominate the nuances in the different ways of speaking, even their accents when speaking in English. To the annoyance of my family members, I would take on the challenge of perfecting these characters while at home. But I never did it with a career in mind; much to my surprise, that came later, after my twenty-third birthday, in the most unexpected and random way.

It was around March 2013. I was visiting a friend who was in the hospital when her sister happened to ask me if I'd heard of an app called Vine. I hadn't. She showed it to me, and I thought it looked fun, so I downloaded it. There was no lightbulb moment, no thought bubble above my head saying, *That's it! I'm going to be a Viner!* It was a cool pastime, something new to check out, and it played into my love of making home videos when I was a kid. I had no idea that app would alter the course of my career and life.

At the time, I was living on my own in a scrappy little apartment in a shady part of town, which was all I could afford. After having worked for a few months as a bell dispatcher at Disney when I was sixteen, I switched over to retail and got my first job at Nike as a sales associate. In my mind, it was a match made in heaven, because it brought me closer to the sports-related career I dreamed about and fed into my passion for sneakers. I slowly worked my way up at the store, and eventually became a retail manager. That's when I decided to pursue my career at Nike instead of getting a four-year college degree. My parents were skeptical, but I was determined to make it in this company and steadily work my way up the corporate ladder. It wasn't my dream job yet, but I thought I could eventually make something more of it. I knew it was an unconventional route to take. My mom's doubts and questions about this decision fed my own concerns. There were no guarantees, but I didn't let these thoughts dishearten me. I had faith that I could make it work.

I spent most of my time at the store, and when I wasn't working, I was usually at home. I had no girlfriend and wasn't into going out, so I started using Vine more often to let my creative spirit take flight through those six-second videos. The app was only a few months old, I was the first Hispanic to pick up a large following, and I hopped on right before Vine became 2013's fastest-growing app in the world. I hit the jackpot and I didn't even know it. I was just having a good time creating short-form videos that made people laugh.

Meanwhile, word started spreading that there was a Hispanic dude posting funny Vines, and Viners started gravitating toward my account, which only grew further when the ReVine button was added to the app, and received an even bigger boost when Twitter acquired Vine. Suddenly, my Vines went from posts I shared with friends and some followers to posts that were Re-

Vined and also shared and retweeted on Twitter. Some people liked what I was doing so much, or were so intrigued by my sudden following, that they started imitating my videos. *This is crazy!* I thought, as I saw it all unfold before my eyes. We're talking about a time when social media influencers didn't exist yet. Many of us were still on the cusp of discovering that our favorite pastime could actually be considered entertainment and a serious business tool.

I didn't know what I was doing at first. The truth is I didn't really use social media much other than to communicate with friends. It wasn't my source of entertainment, but that slowly changed. I began to follow other people and tune in to what my followers reacted to the most, and I quickly realized it was my original content, rather than my ReVines of things I found funny. They were most into the six-second spots where I acted out scenes from my childhood about being Hispanic in the United States. It came naturally to me, and it clearly struck a chord with my growing audience. I honestly didn't see it as a moneymaking opportunity. What I loved about it was that I was making people laugh and connecting with them via these childhood moments that all of us as Hispanics have experienced in some form.

I specifically remember one day when my parents swung by my place to pick me up and, awestruck by the growing popularity of my posts, I decided to share the phenomenon with them. I eagerly handed them the phone and explained it all while they watched some of the videos, expecting a big reaction. But they didn't quite get it. They handed back my phone and said something like *"Qué bueno, hijo,* that's nice," as if I'd shown them pictures of a recent vacation. While I was amazed at the following I was amassing, they made nothing of it, unaware of how this would eventually affect their own lives too. I always marvel at how things unfold and how God really does work in mysterious ways.

Instagram was already pretty popular by then, so one day I decided to share my handle with my Vine and Twitter followers, and in a matter of an hour I went from a few thousand followers to fifty thousand. I couldn't believe my eyes. My heart was pounding with excitement. It was clear that I had tapped into something important, I just wasn't sure what to do about it. So I kept going, ecstatic that I was able to hit so many people's funny bones. With fifty thousand followers, I thought I was super popular and famous and had totally made it. It was like going from being the coolest kid on the block to being the coolest kid in the city.

However, while my social media life was thriving, my real life had taken somewhat of a nosedive. I was unhappy at work, but that was my bread and butter. Instead of pursuing a bachelor's degree, I had deposited all my hopes for a career in that one place. I had invested six years in the company, but it wasn't all I had hoped it would be. The following five to six months were torturous. I fulfilled my job requirements, but my heart was no longer in it. I toyed with the idea of leaving, but I didn't have much else going for me and no clear exit strategy, so I stuck it out awhile longer. The clock became my best friend. As soon as it struck closing time, I would bolt out of there like the Flash.

I was lodged between a rock and a hard place, passing through one of the toughest and unhappiest times of my life, and that's when my social media status began to take off. Coworkers followed me on Vine, customers who came into the store started recognizing me: "Oh, you're the guy from Vine! Can I get a picture with you?" *What? A picture with me?* I couldn't believe it. What was going on? It started happening so frequently that my manager pulled me aside one day and said, "Listen, Juan, this is getting out of hand." He thought all the picture taking was a distraction in the workplace, so I was instructed to step outside each time I was asked for a photo. This kind of backfired on the store staff when they realized that my stepping outside became so frequent that it started interfering with my work. Then I got a warning to be careful about what I put online as it could reflect badly on the company. Nothing I posted was defamatory or detrimental to anyone, but their fear that I might cross a line pushed management to deliver their final ultimatum. I was called in to my manager's office and told, "We're happy that this is happening to you, but it's time to make a decision. You either stop this Internet thing and focus on your job here as shipping and handling department manager, or focus on social media full-time. But you can't do both."

It was the end of summer 2013. I was not in college, my mom was questioning what I was doing with my life, I was no longer really happy at work, and I honestly had nothing going for me except for this fun social media adventure. And that's when it hit me. I woke up one day and realized I was tired of investing so much of my time and energy in someone else's brand. In my twenty-three-year-old mind, it was a no-brainer. I quit my job and took the biggest leap of faith in my life, with no backup plan and no real future plan either. All I knew was that I couldn't continue living like that. I chose to stop settling for a nine-to-five job that wasn't fulfilling me and instead pursue my dream.

That evening, I got home with three thousand dollars in my bank account and a dream I wasn't quite sure how I was going to achieve. I had just quit my job, had nothing going on on the education front, had no love life to speak of, and although I was somewhat terrified, my heart was pounding with excitement and possibility. For the first time in a long time, I felt alive again. I was ecstatic, even though a few weeks into this adventure, I hit a major reality check. I could no longer afford my car payments, and I desperately needed to cut costs to stretch out my savings, so I had to let my car get repossessed. *There goes my credit.* It was horrible, but I pressed on. My former coworkers were making fun of my decision, certain it was naïve of me to think I could make a living off of my six-second Vine videos. But that didn't stop me either. I put my faith in God and used it to propel myself forward. It was a tough and strange time in my life. I had my doubts—*If I fail, all of this will have been for nothing*—but deep inside there was a voice telling me that something had to give. At the end of the day, it was really up to me to grab my future and steer it in a new direction, *con la bendición de Dios,* of course.

When my parents found out about my impulsive decision, they totally freaked out. "*¿Estás seguro, hijo?* Are you sure? You're leaving your job for this?" I pleaded my case, and although they didn't quite approve, they stood by me, likely worried about when the other shoe would drop.

So now what? My savings wouldn't last forever. I would be lucky if it got me through a full two months of rent, bills, and food. The clock was ticking, and I wasn't sure what I would do, until I got offered an opportunity to host a two-hour event at a nightclub. It paid five hundred dollars, so I jumped at the chance. Even though these hosting gigs were few and far between at the time, I managed to scrape by. I spent those first few months eating hot dogs, sandwiches, and cereal as my main meals to cut corners, and I prayed nonstop. My siblings were doing great, following their educational paths, and I couldn't have been happier for them, but I also couldn't help comparing what I was doing to all of their accomplishments and feeling that I was falling short of my parents' expectations. To be honest, although I was following my heart, I was also very lost, so I braced myself and latched on to my faith—*Something's gotta work out for me*—and eventually, it did.

I spent the following year racking up hosting gigs that had me traveling around the country. My social media following continued to grow, but what people didn't really understand was that I wasn't a stand-up comedian. When I walked onstage, the audience assumed that the minute the mic was in my hands, I would bust out into a set filled with rib-cracking jokes. But that isn't me—I've never done stand-up in my life! Ricky Padilla—my manager from the start, one of the first people to believe in me and guide me through my career—would break it down to the promoters and explain that rather than jokes, my presence could be used more like a meet-and-greet scenario. No one quite got it, but I'd get booked nonetheless and would show up, take pictures for a certain amount of time, and then hang out with everyone in the club's VIP area. It was basically a "Come party with Le-Juan" setup, although I've never been much of a partier. But hey, a job's a job, and if it allowed me to do what I loved and connect with my audience, I was game.

The hosting gigs kept coming, my fee started to climb with my popularity, and I suddenly felt like things were trending upward. The days of living on hot dogs with a repossessed car seemed light-years away. Now I was hopping on planes to the West Coast, East Coast, the Midwest, the South, I was getting paid cash, my following was growing, and I felt like I had made it. It was any social media influencer's dream.

After the hosting gig demand skyrocketed, the brands came calling. A marketing company based in California reached out to me saying that T-Mobile wanted to partner with social media influencers. The idea was to send us to *Premios Juventud* to create content and post it on our accounts as a paid sponsorship. The fee: $7,500. *Oh . . . my . . . God!* I thought that was it! I couldn't believe it. *I done did it! I'm rich! The only way is up!* I still have a partnership with T-Mobile today. They were the first company to take a chance on me, and I will never forget that.

Other brands followed, and I suddenly understood how this whole social media career actually worked. Brands want to tap into your network of followers, so they reach out to see if you'd be interested in promoting their campaigns. It was basic marketing, the stuff I had learned back in community college. Once I got this, I took a harder look at what I had been doing and realized that it was time to make a change. I needed my actions to reflect my family-friendly comedy, and those hosting gigs weren't cutting it. Slowly, I let go of them and continued to focus on my content, my message, my purpose: to make families laugh. That's ultimately what makes me the happiest at what I do.

The truth is that the social media influencer world is incredibly unpredictable. No one can tell you how long something like this can last. There are absolutely no guarantees. One day you're in, the next you're out. The apps can disappear as quickly as they came onto the scene, and you can be left with nothing. To keep my head on straight and not lose my sanity with all the what-ifs, I just focus on what I love and take it one day at a time. Under any other circumstances, this would have made me feel incredibly uneasy, but by this time I was dating Camila, and her unwavering support and encouragement kept me going. She gave me the strength to pursue my dreams and follow my gut, and with her by my side, that's exactly what I did.

By 2014, I had stopped the night-venue hosting gigs completely and was focused on creating content and partnering up with brands that accurately reflected LeJuan James. I still can't believe how blessed I am. Every day I wake up grateful for every experience, both good and bad, that has led me to become who I am today. I'm thrilled with what I've accomplished and am at ease growing at a slow and steady pace; this approach has let me make better decisions, and it gives me the space and time to create content that you will enjoy and appreciate and that I am proud of sharing. God smiled down on me once again, together with my abuela Carlita, who had already joined Him, and allowed me to continue on this path to make kids, teens, parents, and grandparents laugh and to truly make a positive difference in people's lives.

## Behind the Scenes

I don't write things down. I mull over an idea that pops into my head, or sit down for brainstorming sessions with Camila, until I can visualize the story line and feel in my gut that it's the one I want to produce as a short-form video. Then I cast the characters, explain the premise, and get to work. Much like comedic improvisation, my videos are completely unscripted, but I know exactly what tone and message I want to deliver, so while Camila films the scenes, I direct the shoots. If my family is involved, all the better, although they sometimes do get mad at how nitpicky I can be when something isn't coming out the way I envisioned. The thing is, I have this crystal-clear picture in my head of what I want to portray, and I will work tirelessly until I get it right. It can be challenging, but at the end of the day, we always make it work and have a laugh along the way.

With my mom it's actually pretty easy, because many times we're acting out scenes from our own relationship. Since we've been there and done that, the words flow seamlessly from our mouths; it comes naturally to us both, and I think that's why it always feels so authentic. My mom is a star in her own right. I don't remember when she first started appearing in my videos, but she loves the Internet and Facebook so much that when I asked her if she would play a particular character, she was all in. She didn't care if she looked crazy, she was having fun with her son. Eventually, people started gravitating to our videos together, instantly drawn in by her genuine candor, and now she even has her own following.

Something similar happened with Camila. I knew how talented she was and I couldn't wait to help share her skills with the world. She had such incredible potential that I encouraged her to take the plunge. Social media wasn't her thing (she only had about nine hundred followers when we met, and all of her accounts were private), she never needed that type of attention—one of the things I love about her—but when she got her toes wet, she realized how much fun it is to interact and communicate with her audience. She's carved out her own niche now, sharing beauty tricks and important life lessons full of inspiration and warmth. When they first catch a glimpse of her incredible charm, people immediately love her, and I couldn't be more proud of everything she is accomplishing.

I keep getting all of these amazing breaks in my life, and I thank God and Abuela Carlita up above for every single one of them. I know how blessed I am, and even though sometimes it's hard for me to live in the moment, because I'm always busy planning what's to come next, I never want to take any of what happens to me on a daily, weekly, monthly, and yearly basis for granted. I like to sit back, reflect, take it all in, and never forget to be grateful for my life today. My Hispanic *crianza* has helped keep me grounded along the way. If anything ever goes to my head and I start acting like I'm all that, my mom, dad, siblings, and fiancée will quickly bring me down to reality, and I wouldn't have it any other way. I know I am blessed to be surrounded by people who truly love me and want the best for me. This keeps me sane and focused.

I honestly don't need much to be happy other than my loved ones by my side. What defines me is my purpose, not how much money I have in the bank. I like waking up and having something to look forward to in my day, the challenge, the creativity, the satisfaction that comes with making something from scratch, like my videos, and seeing people's joyful reactions. I never want to be in a position where I am too comfortable—that's when you become complacent, creativity's worst enemy—I just want to continue to find creative ways to make people laugh.

If new opportunities arise that are meant to be, they will be. Nothing in my life has been forced, but that doesn't mean I don't push myself to aim for the stars. That's why I'm constantly asking myself, *Okay, so what's next?* Honestly, I see myself as more of an entrepreneur than a famous face on TV; I just happen to have found a path that allows me to invest in side businesses I'm passionate about while also expressing my creative side in the public eye. But by far, my main focus, my purpose, my calling is to continue to make a positive impact on people's lives while I'm here.

I can't tell you how many people have shared their stories with me online and in person about how my videos have positively affected their days and lives. I had no idea I had the power to change someone's outlook until I started getting their live feedback. I'm often stopped on the street, hugged, and sometimes I'm even brought to tears. Like the time I was at a mall and an abuelito in a wheelchair recognized me and started to cry as his daughter wheeled him over to me. He told me he suffered pain on a daily basis and was undergoing chemo, but my videos always managed to cheer him up. It was such a touching and unexpected moment that I couldn't help but cry too.

Another moment I will never forget is when I surprised Jenny, a fan with brain cancer. Her son, Matthew, had reached out to see if I could send her a video with some words of encouragement, but I was so moved by his message and a particular line he wrote—"She watches your videos every day and she laughs like crazy and it keeps her spirits up and seeing her laugh like that in our situation means the world to me"—that I knew I had to meet her. When she came around the corner of her living room and found me standing there, she gasped, started crying, and immediately gave me a warm and loving hug, followed by another hug for my mom, who was standing a few feet away. Tears rolled down my cheeks as I heard her words fill the air, and memories of my own grandmother battling cancer flashed before my eyes.

Understanding just how far-reaching these videos are, how they can change someone's day or distract someone from pain and put a smile on people's faces when they most need it, that has made an enormous impact on my own life. I have found my purpose. I thank God every day for allowing me to build the courage to take a leap of faith and chase my dreams. I believe

I'm a tool of God, put on this planet to bring happiness and positivity to people when they need it most, and I am determined to continue fulfilling this calling.

Choosing to venture down an unconventional path takes not only faith, but tireless hard work, perseverance, and passion. If you're not passionate about what you're doing, you probably won't get very far. Passion fuels you through the days when you want to give up, and, believe me, you will have them. But if you listen to your heart, the possibilities are endless. Is success guaranteed? No. But if you fall down, just pick yourself up, dust yourself off, and keep going. I would rather live my life knowing that I gave it a shot than regretting never having had the courage to take that leap of faith.

To all of you who have sheltered dreams and are constantly being told that you can't make them realities, I'm here to tell you that you can. What makes me so different from you? I was just a kid from Orlando, Florida, a minority whose odds were statistically stacked against him, but that didn't stop me from following my heart. Don't let your current situation dictate your future. Never let fear and doubt overcome your true dreams. I hope we can continue to grow, learn, reminisce, and laugh together. With my family and the love of my life by my side, and you, my dear and loyal audience, pushing me forward and inspiring me to make a positive impact on the world, the sky is the limit. *Lo demás está en las manos de Dios.*

# ACKNOWLEDGMENTS

After writing this book, I think it goes without saying that I would not be where I am today without my parents, Juan and Ingrid; my siblings, Bryan and Nahil; and my fiancée, Camila—thank you for the constant and unconditional love, understanding, and support.

I also want to take this opportunity to thank everyone who has made *Definitely Hispanic* possible. To my manager, Ricky Padilla, and my agent, Eve Attermann, thank you for your guidance and encouragement. To Johanna Castillo, thank you for welcoming me into the Simon & Schuster family. To Melanie Iglesias Pérez, my editor, thank you for your thoughtful ideas and feedback, and your tireless work behind the scenes putting all the pieces of this book puzzle together. To Cecilia Molinari, thank you for interpreting my thoughts and sense of humor and reflecting them so clearly on these pages.

And, last but never least, to my fans and followers, your laughter brightens every one of my days—thank you for your help in making my dream a reality.

# Connect with LeJuan on

**f** TeamLeJuanJames

**𝕏** @LeJuan__James

**◉** @LeJuanJames

**▶** LeJuanJames